# BIBLE
# TREK

## A BOLD TRIVIA JOURNEY
## THROUGH SPACE AND TIME

### JOHN HUDSON TINER

BARBOUR
PUBLISHING

*This book is dedicated to*
*Cheyenne Marie Tiner*

Print ISBN 978-1-61626-693-6

eBook Editions:
Adobe Digital Edition (.epub) 978-1-60742-836-7
Kindle and MobiPocket Edition (.prc) 978-1-60742-837-4

Published by Barbour Publishing, Inc., P.O. Box 719, Uhrichsville, Ohio 44683 www.barbourbooks.com

*Our mission is to publish and distribute inspirational products offering exceptional value and biblical encouragement to the masses.*

Member of the
Evangelical Christian
Publishers Association

Printed in the United States of America.

# BIBLE

# TREK

# CONTENTS

## PREFLIGHT BRIEFING

Welcome to *Bible Trek*, an exciting and challenging voyage through the entire Bible. Each voyage will be a test of your Bible knowledge. A simple scoring system will reveal whether you traveled at maximum Warp Speed or were delayed by a Tractor Beam. Each voyage provides a way to increase your Bible knowledge while having fun.

In some voyages you'll make a difficult trek with a person from the Bible as he or she faces unexpected dangers. Some are heroes who muster courage in the face of fearful circumstances. Others are pursued by imaginary terrors and follow their fears rather than the will of God. In the end, they must choose between truth and lies, between courage and flight.

Distance is not the only challenge a voyage may face. You'll be along for the battle as heroes of faith confront rivals whose goals are contrary to God's plan. You'll meet men of principle and women of honor who face the challenge of a nemesis they must defeat before the voyage can be successfully concluded. Some heroes face powerful and obstinate rulers, while others are the targets of devious schemers.

Still other voyages are interrupted by a Temporal Jump from an event in the Old Testament to a similar event in the New Testament. Unlike treks that are limited in time and scope, a Temporal Jump throws you into the minds of prophets who lived in the past but saw into the future. Many of the prophecies of the Old Testament remained a mystery until the time of the New Testament when the meaning of the prophecy was fully revealed.

Prepare now for the 30 voyages of discovery. You'll make difficult treks, battle nemeses, encounter Temporal Discontinuities, and in one trek you'll make a Quantum Leap.

Unique in each Bible trek is a Black Hole question. Some of the Black Hole questions are an easy way to increase your speed. But others could set you back because a wrong answer requires you to deduct points and may drop you from Light Speed to Impulse Drive. Read the scoring guide, then take your duty post, charge the thrusters, and prepare for an exciting adventure!

## ARRIVAL AT YOUR DEEP SPACE DESTINATION

### SCORING GUIDE

Except for the Black Hole question, a correct answer is one point with no deduction for being incorrect. For the Black Hole question a correct answer is three points, but an incorrect answer deducts one point.

**12 OR MORE POINTS**—You traveled at Maximum Warp Speed.

*8–11  POINTS*—You traveled through hyperspace at Light Speed.

*4–7  POINTS*—You slowed to Impulse Speed. You must have hit a spatial anomaly that slowed you down. Refer to your Commander's orders—holy scripture—to engage the Warp Drive and reset the ship's course toward your destination.

*3 OR FEWER POINTS*—You must have got caught in a Tractor Beam. You have been delayed along the way and are lost in deep space. I'm happy to tell you this trek is not over. Review your answers and power up for the next destination. Remember the loving Father restores those to the correct destination who are determined to remain faithful.

Note: The answers for each voyage follow the final question of that voyage. All Bible quotes, unless otherwise indicated, are from the New International Version. Bible references that appear in **bold** in the answer key signify that the question and/or the answer is a direct quote from the scriptures.

# BIBLE TREK

# VOYAGE 1

## TO A FAR COUNTRY

Prepare for the first voyage—a long but important one. You'll join a man who journeys to several different locations, increasing in wealth and respect as he goes. More importantly, his faith in God grows ever stronger. Read the Captain's Log to learn about this trek. Then engage the Warp Drive and be on your way!

### CAPTAIN'S LOG

In your first Bible trek, you will follow a man who made his home in the Promised Land although he was a stranger to that land. From him would come descendants as numerous as the stars in the sky. The New Testament (Hebrews 11:8–12) lists him as a man of faith.

Voyage 1 takes you to the Promised Land with _____ and his wife, _____.

**1.** Abram (Abraham) and his family were from _____ of the Chaldeans.

**2.** How many children did Abram and Sarai (Sarah) have before leaving their home country?

**3.** What was Abram's relationship to Lot?

   a. brother
   b. father
   c. friend
   d. uncle

**4.** God told Abram, "All peoples on earth will be _____ through you."

**5.** Why did Abram leave Canaan for Egypt?

   a. there was a famine in Canaan
   b. God directed him to do so
   c. he was searching for an Egyptian maiden to have his child
   d. the Canaanites drove him out

**6.** True or False: Abram feared Pharaoh would want Sarai because of her great wealth.

**7.** How did Abram describe his relationship with Sarai so Pharaoh would not kill him?

**8.** How did Pharaoh treat Abram?

a. shamefully
b. well

**9.** What event caused Pharaoh to realize that Abram was married to Sarai?

a. a plague of locusts descended on Egypt
b. God gave Pharaoh's chief servant a vision
c. Pharaoh was inflicted with serious diseases
d. Sarai admitted the truth

**10.** True or False: When Pharaoh learned of Abram's deception, he released Abram freely but held Sarai for ransom.

**11.** Why did Abram's and Lot's herdsmen quarrel?

**12.** Who suggested that Abram and Lot part company?

**13.** After they parted, Abram lived in Canaan, but Lot pitched his tents near the city of

_____.

**14.** In addition to being husband and wife, how else were Abram and Sarai related?

a. they both were descended from David
b. they had the same father
c. they had the same mother
d. they were cousins

**15.** True or False: Abraham also concealed from Abimelek king of Gerar that Sarah was his wife.

# BLACK HOLE:

True or False: The cave Abraham bought to bury Sarah was owned by a Hittite.

# VOYAGE 1

■■■■■■

## ANSWERS

Abraham (Abram) and Sarah (Sarai) (Genesis 17:5, 15)

1. Ur (Genesis 11:31)
2. none, she was barren (Genesis 11:30)
3. d. uncle (Genesis 11:27)
4. "blessed" **(Genesis 12:3)**
5. a. there was a famine in Canaan (Genesis 12:10)
6. False—it was because of her great beauty (Genesis 12:11–12)
7. that Sarai was his sister (Genesis 12:13)
8. b. well (Genesis 12:16)
9. c. Pharaoh was inflicted with serious diseases (Genesis 12:17)
10. False—he sent both on their way (Genesis 12:20)
11. the land could not support both Abram's and Lot's flocks and herds (Genesis 13:5–6)
12. Abram (Genesis 13:8–9)
13. Sodom (Genesis 13:12)
14. b. they had the same father (Genesis 20:12)
15. True (Genesis 20:2)

Black Hole: True (Genesis 23:5, 16)

## VOYAGE 1

# WELCOME TO YOUR DEEP SPACE DESTINATION

Congratulations on finishing the first voyage. Check your score, one point for each correct answer for the first 15 questions with no penalty for being incorrect. The Black Hole question counts as three points if answered correctly—but deduct one point if you miss it.

Abram lived in Ur of the Chaldeans (modern-day Iraq) with his wife, Sarai, his father, Terah, and nephew Lot. Ur was a wealthy city with imposing buildings and a well-developed culture. Water from the Euphrates River made the land fertile. Yet Abram abandoned these comfortable surroundings for the land promised to him by God. Despite his wife's barrenness, he was told he would become the father of nations.

Abram's travels took many turns both before and after he settled in the Promised Land. In the same way, his faith in God's promise of a male heir also had unexpected twists and turns. We'll follow that epic journey in the next voyage.

> *"Produce fruit in keeping with repentance.*
> *And do not think you can say to yourselves,*
> *'We have Abraham as our father.'*
> *I tell you that out of these stones God*
> *can raise up children for Abraham."*
> MATTHEW 3:8–9

# BIBLE
# TREK

# VOYAGE 2

■ ■ ■ ■ ■ ■ ■

## OUTCAST

In this voyage you'll follow the plight of a servant woman and her son. Hagar had served her mistress Sarai for ten years after Abram left Egypt (Genesis 16:3). Sarai was barren and also past childbearing years. Yet God had promised Abram that he would become the father of many nations. Hagar is improperly enlisted to fulfill this promise. Consult the Captain's Log to discover where this voyage will take you.

### CAPTAIN'S LOG

In this exciting adventure, you'll discover that Abram's firstborn son did not come from Sarah, but from Hagar the servant woman. Some years after the birth of Abram's son by Hagar, God renames Abram "Abraham" and Sarai "Sarah" (Genesis 17:5, 15). The decision for Hagar to be the mother of Abraham's child eventually caused her and her son to be outcasts on a dangerous desert trek. Mother and son survived that challenge and became part of the enduring legacy of world history.

Voyage 2 follows the life of Hagar and her son, _____.

**1.** How did Hagar serve Sarah?

 **2.** What was Hagar's nationality?

 **3.** Who suggested that Abraham have a child by Hagar?

    a. Abraham
    b. an angel of the Lord
    c. Hagar
    d. Sarah

 **4.** When she was pregnant with Ishmael, why did Hagar flee into the desert?

    a. Abraham said her child would never be blessed
    b. Sarah mistreated her
    c. Hagar feared her child would be put to death
    d. Hagar wanted Ishmael to be raised in Egypt

**5.** While Hagar was in the desert at a spring, who told her to go back to Sarah?

    a. an emissary from Abraham
    b. an angel of the Lord
    c. a man in a dream
    d. a donkey that talked

**6.** God told Abraham that every male who is _____ days old must be circumcised.

**7.** True or False: Unlike Abraham and Isaac, Ishmael was never circumcised.

**8.** What was Abraham's reaction when he was told he would have a son by Sarah?

**9.** True or False: Abraham asked for Ishmael to live under God's blessing.

**10.** What event were Abraham and Sarah celebrating when Ishmael was seen to be mocking?

   a. Isaac was being weaned
   b. Isaac was celebrating his thirteenth birthday

**11.** When Sarah told Abraham to "get rid of that slave woman and her son," how did Abraham react?

   a. he was distressed
   b. he was relieved

**12.** True or False: Abraham provided nothing to Hagar and Ishmael as they were sent into the desert of Beersheba.

**13.** Why did Hagar separate herself from Ishmael after the water was gone?

**14.** True or False: Ishmael was with Isaac when they buried Abraham.

**15.** In the New Testament, Paul writes, "We are not children of the _____ woman, but of the _____ woman" (two words).

# BLACK HOLE:

Ishmael is described as using what weapon?

   a. bow and arrow
   b. sling
   c. spear
   d. sword

# VOYAGE 2

■ ■ ■ ■ ■ ■ ■

## ANSWERS

Ishmael (Genesis 16:15)

1. as her slave (Genesis 16:1)
2. Egyptian (Genesis 16:1)
3. d. Sarah (Genesis 16:2)
4. b. Sarah mistreated her (Genesis 16:6)
5. b. an angel of the Lord (Genesis 16:9)
6. eight (Genesis 17:12)
7. False—Ishmael was circumcised at age 13 (Genesis 17:23–25)
8. he laughed (Genesis 17:17)
9. True (Genesis 17:18)
10. a. Isaac was being weaned (Genesis 21:8–9)
11. a. he was distressed (**Genesis 21:10**–11)
12. False—he gave them food and water (Genesis 21:14)
13. she could not watch him die (Genesis 21:15–16)
14. True (Genesis 25:9)
15. "slave," "free" (**Galatians 4:31**)

Black Hole: a. bow and arrow (Genesis 21:20)

## VOYAGE 2

■■■■■■■

## WELCOME TO YOUR DEEP SPACE DESTINATION

How did you do? Better than on the previous voyage? Regardless of your score, continue on your Bible trek, because God gives success to those who persevere.

Although Ishmael nearly died in the desert, an angel appeared, showed Hagar a spring, and assured her that Ishmael would not only live but also thrive and become the father of a great nation (Genesis 21:18). Ishmael had 12 sons, and one of his daughters married Abraham's grandson Esau (Genesis 25:13–15; 28:9).

Ishmael's wife came from Egypt (Genesis 21:21). That country was a great nation at the time of Ishmael, and remained so for many more years. Egypt figures in many events in the Bible, both as a place of refuge and a place of danger.

The next voyage, however, follows the plight of Lot as he settles in the plain of Jordan near the city of Sodom. May God be with you, a child of promise, as you embark upon your next trek.

*There is neither Jew nor Gentile,*
*neither slave nor free, nor is there male and female,*
*for you are all one in Christ Jesus.*
*If you belong to Christ, then you are Abraham's seed,*
*and heirs according to the promise.*
GALATIANS 3:28–29

# BIBLE
# TREK

# VOYAGE 3

## ESCAPING THE INFERNO

In this voyage you'll follow the rise and fall of Lot's fortunes after he and Abraham divided up the land. Abraham moved into the hill country. But Lot pitched his tents on the plain of Jordan near the city of Sodom. Later he apparently gave up that shelter for a house in the city itself. The angels sent into the city by God found Lot at the city's gateway (Genesis 19:1). Read the Captain's Log for more details about this voyage.

### CAPTAIN'S LOG

Have you ever entertained an angel? Lot did. In fact, some of those heavenly creatures warned him to flee because of the destruction about to come upon the city. Following Lot's hasty departure, God destroyed Sodom and the other cities on the plain. The angels lead only four people out of the city— Lot and three others, although one dies shortly after the destruction begins.

The three who escape from the city are Lot, his _____ and two _____.

**1.** True or False: During the famine in Canaan, when Abraham went to Egypt, Lot went there, too.

**2.** The Lord told Abraham, "The outcry against Sodom and _____ is so great and their sin so grievous."

**3.** At first, Abraham asked if God would spare Sodom for the sake of how many righteous people?

**4.** At the end, God said that for the sake of _____ righteous people He would not destroy the city.

**5.** How many angels came to visit the city of Sodom?

**6.** After Lot first invited the angels to his home, how did they respond?

   a. they acted as if they were going to another city

   b. they readily agreed

   c. they said, "We will spend the night in the square"

   d. they said, "We'll come at a more convenient time"

**7.** True or False: Lot addressed the mob at the door by calling them "friends."

**8.** What did Lot offer to appease the mob of men at his door who were demanding that Lot send out the two angels?

   a. a choice of his menservants

   b. all that he possessed

   c. his two unmarried daughters

   d. the angels

**9.** What did the angels do to stop the men from breaking down Lot's door?

    a. called down lightning
    b. locked the door and stood before the men
    c. made them act like donkeys eating grass
    d. struck the men blind

**10.** When Lot told the men who were to marry his daughters that the city would be destroyed, how did they react?

    a. they put on sackcloth and ashes and repented
    b. they agreed to leave, but delayed to gather possessions
    c. they left immediately with fear and trembling
    d. they thought Lot was joking

**11.** True or False: Lot needed no urging by the angels to leave the city.

**12.** What happened to Lot's wife when she looked back at the destruction of the city?

**13.** After they escaped into the mountains, where did Lot live?

    a. in land given to him by Abraham
    b. with his two daughters in a cave

**14.** The oldest daughter of Lot had a son named Moab. Who was Moab's father?

**15.** True or False: Jesus said that cities that heard His word and saw His miracles but ignored His teachings would be judged more harshly than Sodom.

# BLACK HOLE:

In addition to doing detestable things before God, Ezekiel writes, "She [Sodom] and her daughters were _____, overfed and unconcerned; they did not help the poor and needy."

## VOYAGE 3

### ANSWERS

wife, daughters (Genesis 19:15–16)

1. True (Genesis 13:1)
2. "Gomorrah" (**Genesis 18:20**)
3. 50 (Genesis 18:24)
4. 10 (Genesis 18:32)
5. two (Genesis 19:1)
6. c. they said, "We will spend the night in the square" (**Genesis 19:2**)
7. True (**Genesis 19:7**)
8. c. his two unmarried daughters (Genesis 19:8)
9. d. struck the men blind (Genesis 19:11)
10. d. they thought Lot was joking (Genesis 19:14)
11. False—he hesitated and the angels had to take him by the hand (Genesis 19:16)
12. "She became a pillar of salt" (**Genesis 19:26**)
13. b. with his two daughters in a cave (Genesis 19:30)
14. Lot himself (Genesis 19:36–37)
15. True (Matthew 10:14–15; Matthew 11:23–24)

Black Hole: "arrogant" (**Ezekiel 16:49**)

# VOYAGE 3

## WELCOME TO YOUR DEEP SPACE DESTINATION

Check your score for this voyage. Did you arrive in first place or struggle to finish? Whether you arrive at Warp Speed or Impulse Power, each voyage provides a way to increase your Bible knowledge. Accept the challenge and set the course for your next deep-space destination.

With the destruction of Sodom and the other cities of the plain, Lot's fortunes took a downward turn. He left the city in haste, being hurried along by the angels. His sons-in-law (pledged to marry his daughters) did not escape the city's destruction, and his wife died along the way. Lot and his two daughters alone survived. As the Bible account ended, he had lost all of his great wealth and lived in a cave.

Your next voyage, Emissary for a Bride, returns to Abraham's family and the search for a proper bride for Isaac.

*Add to your faith goodness; and to goodness, knowledge;*
*and to knowledge, self-control; and to self-control,*
*perseverance; and to perseverance, godliness;*
*and to godliness, mutual affection;*
*and to mutual affection, love.*
2 PETER 1:5–7

# BIBLE

# TREK

# VOYAGE 4

■ ■ ■ ■ ■ ■ ■

## EMISSARY FOR A BRIDE

How did you do in your last voyage? You probably did better in choosing your answers than Lot did in choosing a place to live. Lot's life is a dreadful example to those who make unwise decisions, fall away from the Lord, and then linger in the dark places where life's trek has taken them.

Lot may have delayed leaving Sodom because his wife was from that city. Finding the right spouse can be a challenge. In your next voyage you'll explore how Abraham found a wife for his son and how one of his grandsons married not one, but two, wives. See the Captain's Log for your next assignment.

### CAPTAIN'S LOG

It is time to start another Bible trek. In this voyage you'll set your heading north from Canaan with your goal in northwest Mesopotamia, the previous home of Abraham. You'll follow a servant who goes there to find a bride for Isaac. Later one of Isaac's sons returns to the same place for his own bride.

Isaac's bride was named _____.

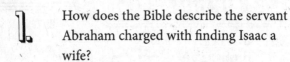

**1.** How does the Bible describe the servant Abraham charged with finding Isaac a wife?

    a. a Canaanite slave of good report
    b. a servant old and wise
    c. a servant trustworthy and true
    d. the senior servant in charge of all Abraham had

**2.** "So the servant put his hand under the _____ of his master Abraham and swore an oath."

**3.** How many camels loaded with gifts did the servant take?

**4.** Rebekah said, "Drink, and I'll water your _____, too."

**5.** What was Laban to Rebekah?

a. her brother
b. her father
c. her guardian warrior
d. her servant

 **6.** True or False: The servant was told to go to Abraham's own clan and family to find a wife for Isaac.

**7.** When asked if she would go with Abraham's servant, how did Rebekah reply?

a. "I am the Lord's handmaiden"
b. "I must have ten days to prepare"
c. "I will go"
d. remained silent and let her mother answer

 **8.** True or False: Isaac was in a field meditating when he first saw Rebekah.

**9.** The twin sons of Isaac and Rebekah were named Jacob and _____.

**10.** When Jacob first saw Rachel, what favor did he do for her?

a. removed the spotted sheep from her flock
b. gave her a nose ring and two bracelets
c. rescued her as other shepherds drove her away when she tried to water her flock
d. rolled a stone away from the well

**11.** Jacob agreed to work _____ years for Rachel, but had to work _____ years.

**12.** Instead of Rachel, Jacob was first given _____ as his wife.

**13.** Jacob's oldest son was named
_____.

**14.** Jacob's sons by Rachel were named
_____ and Benjamin.

**15.** In all, how many sons did Jacob have?

# BLACK HOLE:

Why did Abraham insist that Isaac not leave Canaan?

## VOYAGE 4

■ ■ ■ ■ ■ ■

### ANSWERS

Rebekah (Genesis 24:67)

1.   d. the senior servant in charge of all Abraham had (Genesis 24:2)
2.   "thigh" **(Genesis 24:9)**
3.   10 (Genesis 24:10)
4.   camels (Genesis 24:19)
5.   a. her brother (Genesis 24:29)
6.   True (Genesis 24:4, 38)
7.   c. "I will go" **(Genesis 24:58)**
8.   True (Genesis 24:63)
9.   Esau (Genesis 25:25–26)
10.  d. rolled a stone away from the well (Genesis 29:10)
11.  7, 14 years (Genesis 29:20, 27–28)
12.  Leah (Genesis 29:28)
13.  Reuben (Genesis 29:32)
14.  Joseph (Genesis 35:24)
15.  12 (Genesis 35:22–26)

Black Hole: God had promised Canaan to Abraham's offspring (Genesis 24:6–7)

## VOYAGE 4

■■■□□■■■

# WELCOME TO YOUR DEEP SPACE DESTINATION

Can you imagine your parents selecting a spouse for you? For Abraham, making a good match for Isaac was serious business. Abraham did not want his son's wife to come from the neighboring, idol-serving Canaanites. Yet he did not want the son of promise to leave the Promised Land. Abraham himself was too old to travel. So he gave the senior servant the important task of finding the future bride among Abraham's own family. The route took the servant to Haran, in what is now southern Turkey, where Abraham's family had settled after leaving Ur. The senior servant's route back with Rebekah was even longer. Isaac had moved to the Negev desert, about 50 miles south of Gaza.

Distance is not the only challenge a voyage may face. Along the way, a nemesis can arise to challenge a hero. The duel of individuals with contrary goals happens in your next voyage. Godspeed!

> " 'I am the God of Abraham,
> the God of Isaac, and the God of Jacob.'
> He is not the God of the dead but of the living."
> MATTHEW 22:32

# BIBLE

# TREK

# VOYAGE 5

## RECONCILIATION

Now that you've been debriefed from your previous voyage, it is time to begin the next trek. The life of Isaac is one dominated by others. As a child, he willingly trusted his father, Abraham, who intended to sacrifice him. As an elderly father, he is befuddled as his wife Rebekah and a son scheme to usurp Isaac's firstborn. Read the Captain's Log to learn more about the conflict between Isaac's contentious twins.

### CAPTAIN'S LOG

In this voyage you'll face the challenge of a nemesis who must be overcome before you can continue the voyage. Two brothers fight. One is a deceitful schemer whose actions cause him to flee the Promised Land and live in fear for 20 years (Genesis 31:38). The other seeks immediate gratification and sacrifices a great inheritance for nothing more than a good meal. Prepare now for a voyage not in distance but into the minds of two brothers who each see the other as a nemesis.

Isaac's feuding sons are _____ and _____.

**1.** In speaking to Rebekah about her twin boys, God said, "The _____ will serve the _____."

**2.** Jacob grasped Esau by the _____ as they were born.

**3.** Which phrase best describes Jacob?

   a. a crafty tradesman who grew wealthy in the marketplace
   b. a man who could understand visions and dreams
   c. a homebody who dwelled in tents
   d. a skillful hunter who loved the open country

**4.** True or False: In his old age Isaac could eat only herbs and wild grapes.

**5.** Who said, "Quick, let me have some of that red stew"?

**6.** True or False: The fact that Esau married Hittite (Canaanite) women was a source of grief to both Isaac and Rebekah.

**7.** When Isaac became old and could not see, what request did he make of Esau?

**8.** What animals did Jacob give Rebekah to prepare as a meal for Isaac?

**9.** How did Rebekah help Jacob appear hairy like his brother Esau?

  a. she covered him with rough sackcloth
  b. she got Isaac drunk with wine
  c. she put goatskin on Jacob's hands and neck
  d. she told Jacob to stand a respectful distance from his father

**10.** What did Jacob intend to steal by his deception of Isaac?

    a. his brother's birthright
    b. his father's blessing

**11.** What smell convinced Isaac that Jacob was Esau?

**12.** Where did Jacob go to escape Esau's wrath?

    a. to Egypt
    b. to Ishmael's clan in the desert
    c. to Rebekah's brother, Laban
    d. to the cave where Lot had stayed

**13.** After Jacob's years in fear of Esau, which wife and son did Jacob put at the rear of his company as Esau approached with his 400 men?

**14.** When Esau saw Jacob, he ran and _____ him.

**15.** When offered the present of flocks and herds from Jacob, what did Esau say?

    a. "I already have plenty, my brother"
    b. "I desire kindness, not a guilt offering"

# BLACK HOLE:

True or False: Isaac died before his twin sons were reconciled.

# VOYAGE 5

## ANSWERS

Esau, Jacob (Genesis 25:25–26)

1. "older," "younger" **(Genesis 25:23)**
2. heel (Genesis 25:26)
3. c. a homebody who dwelled in tents (Genesis 25:27)
4. False—he could eat meat, too (Genesis 25:28; 27:1–4)
5. Esau **(Genesis 25:30)**
6. True (Genesis 26:34–35; 28:8)
7. prepare a tasty meal of wild game (Genesis 27:1–4)
8. young goats (Genesis 27:9, 14)
9. c. she put goatskin on Jacob's hands and neck (Genesis 27:16)
10. b. his father's blessing (Genesis 27:10, 27)
11. the scent on Esau's clothes that Jacob wore (Genesis 27:15, 27)
12. c. to Rebekah's brother, Laban (Genesis 27:43)
13. Rachel and Joseph (Genesis 33:1–2)
14. embraced or kissed (Genesis 33:4)
15. a. "I already have plenty, my brother" **(Genesis 33:9)**

Black Hole: False—they both buried him (Genesis 35:28–29)

# VOYAGE 5

## WELCOME TO YOUR DEEP SPACE DESTINATION

How well did you remember the details of this struggle between brothers? Suspense builds as Esau and his men draw closer to Jacob and his family. The description of their reunion is extraordinarily vivid. It is one of the most gripping accounts in the Bible.

Jacob returned home after being away about 20 years. His large party included two wives; two servant women by whom he'd had children; 11 sons; and a daughter, Dinah. Later he and Rachel would have Benjamin, their only son born in the land of promise.

The Bible account of discord between brothers does not end with Esau and Jacob. The 12 sons of Jacob are not entirely thrilled with the favoritism Jacob shows for one of their number. That antagonism leads to another great clash. May peace be with you and yours as you undertake your next Bible trek!

*Be joyful in hope, patient in affliction, faithful in prayer. Share with the Lord's people who are in need. Practice hospitality. Bless those who persecute you; bless and do not curse. Rejoice with those who rejoice; mourn with those who mourn. Live in harmony with one another.*
ROMANS 12:12–16

# BIBLE
# TREK

# VOYAGE 6

■ ■ ■ ■ □ ■ ■

## TREACHERY

■ □ ■ □ ■

Did your latest trek carry any unexpected questions? Most voyages do have a twist or two, which can be easily overcome. The challenge occurs when problems follow one after another, each growing severer than the last. That certainly happened to the main character in this adventure. It's an account with suspense, exploits, and a happy ending. Refer to the Captain's Log to learn more about this hero of faith and the nemesis he faced.

### CAPTAIN'S LOG

Even as a teenager, this hero was a person of honesty, integrity, and principle. But as we all know, not everyone honors a person of principle. The main character's half brothers sold him into slavery in Egypt. His master's wife falsely accused him. His prison mate—whom he had helped by interpreting a dream—promptly forgot him once freed from prison. In the end, however, all turned out well, not only for this hero but for his family and a nation as well. Take another great ride through history. . . .

Follow _____ as his half brothers sell him into slavery, after which he is taken to Egypt.

**1.** What special gift did Jacob give his son Joseph?

    a. a pearl of great price
    b. a decorative robe
    c. gold, balm, and myrrh
    d. his signet ring showing authority

**2.** In Joseph's dream, what did his brothers' sheaves of grain do to his sheave?

**3.** When Joseph approached, the brothers said to each other, "Here comes that _____! . . . Let's kill him."

**4.** Who objected when the brothers planned to kill Joseph?

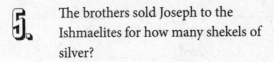
**5.** The brothers sold Joseph to the Ishmaelites for how many shekels of silver?

    a. 20
    b. 30
    c. 40
    d. 70

**6.** How did the brothers convince their father that Joseph was dead?

**7.** Of the two men in prison whose dreams Joseph interpreted, which one was restored to his job?

    a. the baker
    b. the cupbearer

**8.** In Pharaoh's dream, what type of fat and sleek animals stood on the bank of the Nile?

**9.** In Pharaoh's dream, the _____ scorched, worthless heads of grain represented _____ years of famine (same word).

**10.** True or False: Joseph was put in charge of all Egypt except for the throne, which Pharaoh reserved for himself.

**11.** On the first trip, how many brothers came to Egypt?

**12.** On the first trip, what accusation did Joseph make against his brothers to frighten them into telling him more about his father and family?

a. they had stolen grain
b. they used false weights and measures
c. they were spies
d. they worshipped false gods

**13.** True or False: After being away for so long, Joseph could not understand his brothers and had to use an interpreter.

**14.** Joseph told his brothers, "It was not you who sent me here, but _____."

**15.** On the second trip for grain, who else came with the brothers?

    a. Benjamin
    b. Jacob
    c. both Jacob and Benjamin

# BLACK HOLE:

Joseph's family was allowed to settle in the region of _____ in Egypt.

## VOYAGE 6

■■■■■■■

### ANSWERS

Joseph (Genesis 37:28)

1. b. a decorative robe (Genesis 37:3)
2. bowed to it (Genesis 37:7)
3. "dreamer" **(Genesis 37:19–20)**
4. Reuben (Genesis 37:21)
5. a. 20 (Genesis 37:28)
6. they showed him Joseph's robe dipped in goat's blood (Genesis 37:31–33)
7. b. the cupbearer (Genesis 40:21)
8. cows (Genesis 41:18)
9. seven, seven (Genesis 41:27)
10. True (Genesis 41:40–41)
11. 10; Benjamin stayed behind (Genesis 42:3–4)
12. c. they were spies (Genesis 42:9)
13. False—he could understand the language (Genesis 42:23)
14. "God" **(Genesis 45:8)**
15. a. Benjamin (Genesis 43:8–15)

Black Hole: Goshen or the district of Rameses (Genesis 46:34; 47:11)

# VOYAGE 6

## WELCOME TO YOUR DEEP SPACE DESTINATION

Did you finish this voyage on the same up-note as Joseph? Or did you get waylaid in a pit? Joseph understood that, no matter what, the only true course to follow was to continue to trust in God and allow God to show him the way. Joseph himself said that his route to Egypt had been chosen by God and not by his brothers or blind chance.

The seven years of famine were not yet halfway finished when Joseph's father and all his company moved to Egypt. Pharaoh met them and gave Joseph's family the choice land, a region called Goshen where the 70 direct descendants of Jacob (renamed Israel by God) settled (Genesis 46:27). Raising their herds and crops in the best land of Egypt and favored by Joseph and Pharaoh, the children of Israel grew numerous—so numerous that succeeding pharaohs began to fear their power. The next voyage begins a new chapter in the saga of the children of Israel. So let's turn the page!

*This is how we know that we love the children of God:*
*by loving God and carrying out his commands.*
*In fact, this is love for God: to keep his commands.*
*And his commands are not burdensome,*
*for everyone born of God overcomes the world.*
1 JOHN 5:2–4

# BIBLE
# TREK

# VOYAGE 7

■■■■■■

## STEEP LEARNING CURVE

Do you have enough faith and courage to embark upon the next voyage? Moses needed both to return to the great and prosperous empire of Egypt and demand that Pharaoh release the descendants of Jacob. Moses' battle against Pharaoh is mentioned time and again in the Bible. Psalm 105 restates the events in verse form. In Acts 7, Stephen recapped the story in what turned out to be his farewell address. And Hebrews 11 describes Moses as a hero of faith.

### CAPTAIN'S LOG

Pharaoh enjoyed immense influence both within Egypt and outside its borders. In this Bible trek you'll find him a nemesis to be reckoned with. Moses and Aaron met with him first and showed a miracle of God's power. Pharaoh dismissed the demonstration and refused to listen to them. But the series of confrontations had only begun. Pharaoh became a reluctant student of God's power. His obstinance caused his learning curve to be a steep one. May we be wiser than he was.

The steep learning curve included _____ plagues on Egypt.

**1.** At the burning bush, what did God tell Moses to take off?

**2.** God instructed Moses and the elders of Israel to ask Pharaoh, the ruler of Egypt, to let them "take a _____-day journey into the wilderness to offer sacrifices to the LORD."

**3.** How did God demonstrate his power to Moses?

a. He caused Moses' hand to become leprous
b. He caused the sun to stand still for one hour
c. He provided a sacrificial goat with seven horns
d. He turned Moses' staff into gold

**4.** What skill did Moses claim to lack, which God countered by giving that duty to his brother Aaron?

**5.** Who asked, "Who is the LORD, that I should obey him?"

   a. a chief elder of the Israelites, who opposed Moses
   b. a taskmaster of the Israelite slaves
   c. Pharaoh himself
   d. Pharaoh's chief magician

**6.** What did Pharaoh command so the children of Israel would have to work harder?

**7.** True or False: When the work became harder, the Israelites were quick to rally behind Moses because they believed God was with him and not Pharaoh.

**8.** Who was the older brother?

   a. Aaron
   b. Moses

**9.** What was the first plague?

**10.** True or False: Pharaoh's magicians with their secret arts were able to duplicate the plague of frogs.

**11.** What was *not* a plague called on Egypt?

a. blinding light
b. boils
c. hail
d. locusts

**12.** True or False: At one point, Pharaoh agreed to let the men go, but not the women and children.

**13.** The Passover is known by what other name?

a. Festival of Dedication
b. Festival of Tabernacles
c. Festival of Unleavened Bread
d. Pentecost

**14.** True or False: The Israelite people escaped Egypt with nothing but the clothes they could carry.

**15.** For how many years did the Israelite people lived in Egypt?

 a. 70
 b. 430
 c. 969
 d. the Bible does not specify the
    number of years

# BLACK HOLE:

In the New Testament, who was stoned after giving a speech in which he said, "At that time Moses was born, and he was no ordinary child."

# VOYAGE 7

## ANSWERS

10 plagues (Exodus 7:14–12:30)

1. his sandals (Exodus 3:5)
2. "three" **(Exodus 3:18)**
3. a. He caused Moses' hand to become leprous (Exodus 4:6)
4. "I am slow of speech and tongue" **(Exodus 4:10)**
5. c. Pharaoh himself **(Exodus 5:2)**
6. gathering their own straw for making bricks (Exodus 5:6–7)
7. False—they became discouraged and did not listen to Moses (Exodus 6:9)
8. a. Aaron was older by three years (Exodus 7:7)
9. water turned to blood (Exodus 7:19)
10. True (Exodus 8:7)
11. a. blinding light (Exodus 9:9, 23; 10:12)
12. True (Exodus 10:11)
13. c. Festival of Unleavened Bread (Exodus 12:17)
14. False—they left with silver, gold, clothing, flocks, and herds (Exodus 12:34–38)
15. b. 430 (Exodus 12:40)

Black Hole: Stephen **(Acts 6:15; 7:20, 58)**

# VOYAGE 7

## WELCOME TO YOUR DEEP SPACE DESTINATION

How did you do? Answering the questions correctly is good. Looking beyond the questions to the lessons we can take away from the voyage is better.

Moses' trek was not over but was only actually beginning. Moses may have believed that convincing Pharaoh to let his people go was the hard part. If so, he was deeply mistaken. The real test came with the journey to the Promised Land. Coming out of slavery, those he led were so timid that the prospect of a battle made them ready to flee back to Egypt. Each new hardship launched them into a raging tantrum against Moses and against God.

*All of you, clothe yourselves with humility toward one another, because, "God opposes the proud but shows favor to the humble." Humble yourselves, therefore, under God's mighty hand, that he may lift you up in due time.*
1 PETER 5:5–6

# BIBLE
# TREK

# VOYAGE 8

## DESERT TREK

Each Bible trek brings a different challenge. Prepare now for another long journey, not only in distance but also in duration. The voyage does not end until an entire generation of Israelites dies in the desert. The physical course was also a spiritual journey. God designed their desert trek to strengthen the second generation and bring them into a closer and more trusting relationship with Him.

### CAPTAIN'S LOG

Pharaoh second-guesses his decision to release the slaves, asking, "What have we done? We have let the Israelites go and have lost their services!" He and his army chase after them. This trek begins with the Israelites in a frightened huddle, thinking they are trapped against a body of water as Pharaoh's army advances. The trek ends years later when the Israelites' children have developed the courage to cross another body of water and seize the Promised Land. Grab your sandals. It's time to do the desert walk.

The Israelites cross both the _____ Sea and the _____ River on dry land.

**1.** Who said, "You must carry my bones up with you from this place [Egypt]"?

    a. Isaac
    b. Jacob
    c. Joseph
    d. Moses' wife, Zipporah

**2.** When the Egyptian army pursued them, the Israelites said to Moses, "Was it because there were no _____ in Egypt that you brought us to the desert to die?"

**3.** By night the Lord guided the Israelites by a pillar of _____.

**4.** True or False: As the Israelites came near the Red Sea, an angel of the Lord came between them and the army of Egypt.

**5.** How much more manna were the Israelites to gather on the sixth day compared to the other days?

**6.** What food did God provide when the Israelites asked for meat to eat?

**7.** The Israelites would win the battle with the Amalekites provided what took place?

   a. Aaron held up a jar with manna in it

   b. Israelite soldiers blew horns and made a great noise

   c. Joshua held up a sword

   d. Moses lifted up his hands

**8.** What wise counsel did Jethro give to his son-in-law Moses?

   a. how to avoid wearing himself out as a judge over Israel

   b. how to avoid war, because the frightened Israelites might return to Egypt

   c. how to divide the land fairly among the tribes of Israel

   d. how to ensure that the widows received proper treatment

**9.** What false idol did Aaron make for the Israelites as Moses delayed coming down from Mount Sinai?

**10.** About the Israelites, God said, "I have seen these people. . .and they are a _____-_____ people" (hyphenated words).

**11.** After Moses burned the idol, ground it into a powder, and put it in water, he made the people do what?

**12.** When the Lord showed himself to Moses, he said, "You will see my _____; but my _____ must not be seen" (two words).

**13.** Because they were frightened to enter the Promised Land, how many years would the Israelites wander in the desert?

**14.** After the Lord sent venomous snakes, what did Moses make for the people to look upon and live?

**15.** From what mountain did Moses view the Promised Land?

    a. Zion
    b. Horeb
    c. Nebo
    d. Sinai

# BLACK HOLE:

How were the Ten Commandments inscribed on the tablets?

    a. front only
    b. on both front and back

## VOYAGE 8

■ ■ ■ ■ ■ ■

### ANSWERS

Red, Jordan (Exodus 14:22; 15:22; Joshua 3:17)

1. c. Joseph **(Exodus 13:19)**
2. "graves" **(Exodus 14:11)**
3. fire (Exodus 13:21)
4. True (Exodus 14:19)
5. twice as much (Exodus 16:5)
6. quail (Numbers 11:18, 31–32)
7. d. Moses lifted up his hands (Exodus 17:11)
8. a. how to avoid wearing himself out as a judge over Israel (Exodus 18:17–26)
9. golden calf (Exodus 32:2–4)
10. "stiff-necked" **(Exodus 32:9)**
11. drink it (Exodus 32:19, 20)
12. "back," "face" **(Exodus 33:23)**
13. 40 (Numbers 14:9, 33–34)
14. bronze snake (Numbers 21:8)
15. c. Nebo (Deuteronomy 34:1–4)

Black Hole: b. on both front and back (Exodus 32:15)

## VOYAGE 8

■■■■■■■

# WELCOME TO YOUR DEEP SPACE DESTINATION

How well did you do? Some of the Black Hole questions are an easy way to gain extra points. But others set you back. If you missed Voyage 8's Black Hole question, don't feel bad, because it was especially difficult. Even if you've been caught in a Tractor Beam, the next voyage will be an opportunity to regain your speed.

Making a successful voyage depends on choosing faith in God over personal fears. The Israelites had the option of following Moses or those who complained about their situation in the desert. In the end, after a frightening report about the strength of the people who would oppose them, they chose to follow their fears. Moses led them for 40 years until the men of fighting age—who had been too afraid to battle—had died.

You are about to embark on a secret mission—one into enemy territory.

*Cast all your anxiety on him because*
*he cares for you. Be alert and of sober mind.*
*Your enemy the devil prowls around*
*like a roaring lion looking*
*for someone to devour.*
1 PETER 5:7–8

# BIBLE
# TREK

# VOYAGE 9

## SECRET MISSION

Are you ready for another adventure? On this trek, you'll follow the spies on their secret mission into Canaan. The Israelites knew that God had reserved Canaan for them. Joseph had given instructions that his bones were to be brought out of Egypt. When he died his body was embalmed and put in a coffin. During their 430 years in Egypt, Joseph's coffin was a reminder that the Israelites would eventually go home.

### CAPTAIN'S LOG

Your next voyage shadows the two groups of spies who went across the Jordan River into the Promised Land. Both agreed Canaan was a rich and fertile land. Yet all but two men in first group counseled against going into it. Forty years later, the second group of spies entered the land, not to see if it could be won but how best to win it.

Moses sent the first spies into Canaan, and—years later—_____ sent the second group.

**1.** How many men did Moses send to explore Canaan?

**2.** Which question did Moses *not* ask of those sent to explore Canaan?

a. are the people strong or weak?
b. are the towns unwalled or fortified?
c. is the soil fertile or poor?
d. can we take the land?

**3.** How many days did the spies explore the land?

**4.** How did the spies carry the single cluster of grapes?

**5.** The spies said that the land flowed with _____ and _____ (two words).

**6.** After seeing the gigantic people of Canaan, the spies compared themselves to what insect?

**7.** What happened to the men responsible for spreading the bad report about Canaan?

   a. they were bitten by poisonous snakes

   b. the earth opened its mouth and swallowed them

   c. they cried, "Forgive our unbelief"

   d. they died of a plague

**8.** Of the men who explored the land, only Joshua and _____ survived to enter it.

**9.** Because the people would not enter the Promised Land, God said that, except for the two noted above, all those of what age would die in the wilderness?

  a. 2 years or older
  b. 20 years or older
  c. 40 years or older
  d. all except those not yet born

**10.** How did the people respond when Joshua called upon them to cross the Jordan?

  a. "wherever you send us we will go"
  b. "we should choose a leader and go back to Egypt"

**11.** How many spies did Joshua send into Canaan?

**12.** Rahab lived in what part of the city?

**13.** True or False: Rahab reported that the people of her land made sport of the Israelites and their God.

**14.** Where did Rahab hide the spies?

    a. in a papyrus basket
    b. in her vineyard
    c. in the bedclothes of an inner room
    d. under stalks of flax on the roof

**15.** How did the spies escape from the city?

# BLACK HOLE:

How was Rahab to mark her location so that it would be spared when Joshua's army attacked?

# VOYAGE 9

■ ■ ■ ■ ■ ■

## ANSWERS

Joshua (Numbers 13:17; Joshua 2:1)

1. 12 (Numbers 13:2–15)
2. d. can we take the land? (Numbers 13:17–20)
3. 40 (Numbers 13:25)
4. "Two of them carried it on a pole between them" **(Numbers 13:23)**
5. milk, honey (Numbers 13:27)
6. grasshopper (Numbers 13:33)
7. d. they died of a plague (Numbers 14:37)
8. Caleb (Numbers 14:38)
9. b. 20 years or older (Numbers 14:29–30)
10. a. "Wherever you send us we will go" **(Joshua 1:16)**
11. two (Joshua 2:1)
12. in the city wall (Joshua 2:15)
13. False—they feared the Israelites (Joshua 2:9)
14. d. under stalks of flax on the roof (Joshua 2:6)
15. Rahab let them down by a rope through her window (Joshua 2:15)

Black Hole: by tying a scarlet cord in the window (Joshua 2:18)

## VOYAGE 9

■■■■■■■

# WELCOME TO YOUR DEEP SPACE DESTINATION

How'd you score this time around? Were you feeling the triumph of victory—or the agony of defeat? Success comes from thoughtful consideration of the questions and instructions.

Before sending out the spies, Moses gave them a series of instructions: "See what the land is like and whether the people who live there are strong or weak, few or many. What kind of land do they live in? Is it good or bad? What kind of towns do they live in. . .unwalled or fortified? How is the soil. . .fertile or poor?" (Numbers 13:18–20).

The spies came back with the requested information but answered a question Moses had not asked: "Can we take the land?" Only two of the 12 chose faith over fear—Joshua and Caleb. Both survived the 40 years in the desert while all other men of fighting age died. When preparing for their first battle, Caleb was 85 years old (Joshua 14:10) but remained unwavering in his belief that God would give them victory! May you, too, choose faith over fear in all your life challenges.

*Praise be to the God and Father of our Lord Jesus Christ!*
*In his great mercy he has given us new birth into a living*
*hope through the resurrection of Jesus Christ from the dead,*
*and into an inheritance that can never perish, spoil or fade.*
*This inheritance is kept in heaven for you.*
1 PETER 1:3–4

# BIBLE TREK

# VOYAGE 10

■ ■ ■ ■ ■ ■ ■

## RETAKING A LEGACY

In Voyage 10 you will find a satisfying conclusion to the series of Bible treks that began with Abraham, continued through Isaac, Jacob, Joseph, and Moses, and concludes with Joshua. Born a slave in Egypt, Joshua became an aide to Moses. He accompanied Moses partway up Mount Sinai where God gave the Ten Commandments. With the death of Moses in the last chapter of Deuteronomy, Joshua succeeded Moses as commander-in-chief. The new leader's story in the book of Joshua continues immediately following Deuteronomy. Read the Captain's Log to learn the details of this voyage.

### CAPTAIN'S LOG

Joshua and the Israelites crossed the Jordan River to occupy the land that God promised them. They did not have far to go to meet their first resistance. His first target was a walled city five miles west of the Jordan River. Joshua enjoyed an amazing victory over the city, and then he was plunged into a humiliating defeat by a small, unimportant village.

Joshua's first objective was to take the city of

_____ .

**1.** True or False: The Israelites were told to stay close enough to touch the ark of the covenant as they crossed the Jordan.

**2.** The ark of the covenant was carried by priests from the tribe of _____.

**3.** God told Joshua that Israel would know that God was with him as He was with _____.

**4.** What was the condition of the Jordan River?

**5.** When did the Jordan River begin to go dry?

   a. as a strong east wind began blowing
   b. when Caleb said, "God will give us the land if we set our feet on it"
   c. when the ark of the covenant was a great distance away
   d. when the priests' feet touched the water's edge

**6.** Where did the priests carrying the ark stand while all Israel crossed over Jordan?

a. on the spot where they first entered the river
b. in the middle of the Jordan River
c. on a cairn of stones taken from the dry riverbed
d. on the plains of Jericho

**7.** How many stones were used to make the memorial to the river crossing?

**8.** True or False: God stopped supplying the manna from heaven for the Israelites the day that Moses died.

**9.** In all, how many times did Joshua's army march around the walls of Jericho?

**10.** In all, how many times did the men of Joshua's army give a great shout?

**11.** What kind of trumpets did the priest sound?

    a. the horns of bulls, coated with blood
    b. the horns of wild oxen
    c. trumpets of bronze
    d. the horns of rams

**12.** True or False: Rahab alone was saved when Jericho was taken.

**13.** After Jericho's success, the Israelites failed at first to take the small city of

_____.

**14.** Where was Achan's plunder secretly hidden?

**15.** What military tactic did Joshua use to finally take the small city?

a. attacked at night while the city slept
b. laid siege
c. made his army appear larger than it really was
d. set up an ambush

# BLACK HOLE:

True or False: Joshua had been Moses' aide since the former's youth.

# VOYAGE 10

■ ■ ■ ■ ■ ■

## ANSWERS

Jericho (Joshua 6:1–3)

1. False—follow, but not go near it (Joshua 3:4)
2. Levi (Joshua 3:3)
3. Moses (Joshua 3:7)
4. at flood stage (Joshua 3:15)
5. d. when the priests' feet touched the water's edge (Joshua 3:15–16)
6. b. in the middle of the Jordan River (Joshua 3:17)
7. 12 (Joshua 4:3)
8. False—the day after they ate food from the land of Canaan (Joshua 5:12)
9. 13, once each day for six days, seven times on the seventh day (Joshua 6:3–4)
10. once, at the end of the final march (Joshua 6:10, 16)
11. d. the horns of rams (Joshua 6:4)
12. False—she and her family (Joshua 6:23)
13. Ai (Joshua 7:4–5)
14. in the ground inside his tent (Joshua 7:21)
15. d. set up an ambush (Joshua 8:3–4, 21–22)

Black Hole: True (Numbers 11:28)

## VOYAGE 10

■ ■ ■ ■ ■ ■ ■

## WELCOME TO YOUR DEEP SPACE DESTINATION

What was your score? Did you zoom along with 12 or more points or limp into dock with far fewer points? Take heart; those who boldly choose to live by God's word are assured a final, satisfactory result.

This voyage showed that self-satisfaction and sin can lead to defeat. Because of sin in the camp, the Israelites suffered an upsetting defeat at a small town. Joshua dealt first with the sin then laid out a masterful military plan. A portion of his army came against Ai, pretended defeat, broke, and ran. The men of Ai, overconfident at this point, chased the Israelites and left Ai undefended. The rest of Joshua's army took the city, and then an ambush finished the opposing fighters.

Joshua is considered one of the greatest of all Israelite military leaders—his army conquered all of the Promised Land. But other military men showed their might by trusting in God, too. The next voyage proves how a small army under the direction of God can overcome a mighty foe.

*"So do not worry, saying, 'What shall we eat?'*
*or 'What shall we drink?' or 'What shall we wear?'*
*For the pagans run after all these things,*
*and your heavenly Father knows that you need them.*
*But seek first his kingdom and his righteousness,*
*and all these things will be given to you as well."*
MATTHEW 6:31–33

# BIBLE
# TREK

# VOYAGE 11

■ ■ ■ ■ ■ ■ ■

## "NOR THE BATTLE TO THE STRONG"

■ ■ ■ ■

After a time to rest and recharge the thrusters, make ready for a voyage to defeat a new nemesis. The Israelites served God throughout the lifetime of Joshua and the generation that followed. But after that they fell into a distressing pattern. They would bow to other gods and suffer subjection by foreign powers. At the time of this voyage, their nemesis was a strong force that even a powerful army would be hard-pressed to defeat. But God decided to show His power in a unique way. Read the Captain's Log to discover more details about your next adventure.

### CAPTAIN'S LOG

In this voyage, Israel faces the nemesis of foreign raiders. At harvest time, the Midianites and Amalekites would destroy the Israelites' wheat and steal their livestock. But God chose a mighty warrior to come to the rescue.

The leader (or judge) going against the Midianites was _____. (Hint: An organization that places Bibles in hotel rooms is named after him.)

**1.** Between the time of Joshua and Gideon, the female judge who had brought peace to Israel for 40 years was named _____.

**2.** The angel of the Lord who appeared to Gideon said, "The LORD is with you, mighty _____."

**3.** What question did Gideon ask of the Lord?

   a. "if our home is deserving, will your peace rest on it?"

   b. "if the LORD is with us, who can go against us?"

   c. "if the LORD is with us, why has all this happened to us?"

   d. "if we believe in the LORD, will you stay in our house?"

**4.** True or False: Gideon said that he was of the weakest clan in Manasseh, and he was the least in his family.

**5.** When the angel's staff touched it, what happened to the offering that Gideon had prepared?

**6.** Gideon was told to destroy his father's altar to _____ and cut down the Asherah _____ (two words).

**7.** As a first test whether God would save Israel under Gideon's leadership, what was to happen overnight to the wool fleece?

**8.** True or False: Satisfied with the first sign, Gideon gathered his army to defeat the Midianites.

**9.** In reducing Gideon's army, what test eliminated the most number of men?

a. those who were afraid
b. those who got down on their knees to drink

**10.** After the tests, how many men did Gideon have left in his army?

**11.** In the Midianite's dream that Gideon overheard, what happened to the Midianite's tent?

a. a burning lantern consumed it
b. a flood from the Jordan River washed it away
c. a round loaf of barley bread overturned it
d. a statue with feet of clay fell on it

**12.** The Israelite battle cry was "A sword for the LORD and for _____!"

**13.** When did Gideon's army attack?

a. at daybreak
b. at high noon
c. at sunset
d. during the night

**14.** True or False: The men of the tribe of Ephraim were angry that Gideon had not called them when he went to fight the Midianites.

**15.** When the Israelites asked Gideon to rule over them, how did he respond?

a. he reluctantly agreed to do so
b. he said he was exhausted and his grandson would rule instead
c. he said his father, Joash, should rule
d. he said the Lord would rule over them

# BLACK HOLE:

What three items did Gideon's men carry into battle?

## VOYAGE 11

■ ■ ■ ■ ■ ■

### ANSWERS

Gideon (Judges 6:12–14)

1. Deborah (Judges 5:1–31)
2. "warrior" **(Judges 6:12)**
3. c. "If the LORD is with us, why has all this happened to us?" **(Judges 6:13)**
4. True (Judges 6:15)
5. fire consumed it (Judges 6:21)
6. Baal, pole (Judges 6:25)
7. "dew only on the fleece" **(Judges 6:37)**
8. False—he asked for a second sign (Judges 6:39)
9. a. those who were afraid (22,000 of 32,000 left [Judges 7:3])
10. 300 (Judges 7:8)
11. c. a round loaf of barley bread overturned it (Judges 7:13)
12. "Gideon" **(Judges 7:20)**
13. d. during the night (Judges 7:19)
14. True (Judges 8:1)
15. d. he said the Lord would rule over them (Judges 8:22–23)

Black Hole: trumpets, torches (lanterns), jars (Judges 7:19–20)

## VOYAGE 11

# WELCOME TO YOUR DEEP SPACE DESTINATION

Have you been enjoying your voyages? Some followed a person as he or she made both a physical and a spiritual trek. Others, such as this one about Gideon, focused on the heart of an individual who came to accept a difficult task from God. Life in the spiritual sense can be as challenging as any physical effort.

Although Gideon proved to be a mighty warrior, he needed frequent reassurance from God. He asked for a test to confirm that the angle spoke for God. Then, to be assured that Israel's enemies would be delivered into his hands, he asked for two more signs. The final encouragement came when Gideon overheard a Midianite tell a friend about a disturbing dream. The friend interpreted the dream to mean Gideon would defeat the Midianites.

In the next voyage you will meet a hero who, like Gideon, comes against a superior force. Unlike Gideon, he is a strong and confident man who has some character flaws.

*But God chose the foolish things
of the world to the shame the wise;
God chose the weak things of the world to shame the
strong. God chose the lowly things of this world and the
despised things—and the things that are not—to nullify
the things that are, so that no one may boast before him.*
1 CORINTHIANS 1:27–29

# BIBLE
# TREK

# VOYAGE 12

## FEMME FATALE

Your next Bible trek is to southwest Israel where the Philistines have a strong presence. In the previous adventure, Gideon had to deal with raiders coming in from outside Israel. In this voyage, the problem is within. Philistine soldiers attacked the village of Israel, stealing grain, cattle, and even children. The Israelites suffered at the hands of the Philistines for 40 years. Then God granted a man supernatural strength to be a thorn in the side of the Philistines. He was strong but not particularly wise, especially when it came to women. Before departure, check out the Captain's Log below.

### CAPTAIN'S LOG

While visiting the cities of the Philistines, the young man fell in love with a Philistine woman and told his parents, "She's the right one for me" (Judges 14:3). Although the wedding party took place, it ended in anger when his wife revealed the riddle he'd proposed to the young groomsmen at the marriage feast.

This Bible trek explores the events in the life of the strong man named _____.

**1.** True or False: While she was pregnant, Samson's mother was told not to drink wine nor other fermented drink and not to eat anything unclean.

**2.** How did Samson's parents react to his interest in a Philistine bride?

a. they vehemently opposed it and refused to visit her
b. they questioned it but arranged the marriage anyway
c. a Nazirite could not marry
d. they deemed it to be God's will

**3.** Samson's riddle was "Out of the eater, something to eat; out of the _____, something sweet."

**4.** How did the Philistines convince Samson's bride to reveal the answer to Samson's riddle?

    a. they held her younger sister captive
    b. they offered her a reward of silver
    c. they threatened to kill her and her father's household
    d. they threatened to kill Samson

**5.** The answer to Samson's riddle was "What is sweeter than _____? What is stronger than a lion?"

**6.** Because they answered the riddle, Samson said, "If you had not plowed with my _____, you would not have solved my riddle."

**7.** How many sets of clothes did Samson have to provide because of his bet?

**8.** What animals did Samson use to burn the grain fields of the Philistines?

**9.** True or False: Samson's wife was given to another man and then died when the Philistines burned her to death.

**10.** After being turned over to the Philistines by the tribe of Judah, Samson killed a thousand Philistine men with a donkey's _____.

**11.** Samson carried away the gates of what city so he could escape?

a. Bethel
b. Gaza
c. Hebron
d. Jericho

**12.** How many times did Samson mislead Delilah about the source of his strength?

**13.** What job was Samson given while in prison?

**14.** Why did Samson's strength return when he was in prison?

**15.** Samson's captors brought him out as entertainment at a festival to what Philistine god?

    a. Baal

    b. Dagon

# BLACK HOLE:

How many years did Samson lead Israel as a judge?

## VOYRGE 12

■■■■■■

### RNSWERS

Samson (Judges 14:5–6)

1. True (Judges 13:4)
2. b. they questioned it but arranged the marriage anyway (Judges 14:1–5)
3. "strong" **(Judges 14:14)**
4. c. they threatened to kill her and her father's household (Judges 14:15)
5. "honey" **(Judges 14:18)**
6. "heifer" **(Judges 14:18)**
7. 30 (Judges 14:12, 19)
8. foxes (Judges 15:4–5)
9. True (Judges 15:6)
10. jawbone (Judges 15:11–16)
11. b. Gaza (Judges 16:1–3)
12. three (Judges 16:7–17)
13. grinding grain (Judges 16:21)
14. his hair grew back after having been shaved (Judges 16:22)
15. b. Dagon (Judges 16:23–25)

Black Hole: 20 (Judges 16:31)

# VOYAGE 12

## WELCOME TO YOUR DEEP SPACE DESTINATION

Did you feel sorry for both Samson and his first bride? The groomsmen told Samson's new wife that they would burn her and her father's household if she did not discover the answer to Samson's riddle. Her tears gleaned an answer from the strong man. When, in a rage, he returned to his father's house, his bride was given to another man. The unnamed woman died when the Philistines burned her and her father to death.

Later the Philistines bribed Delilah, Samson's last love, to learn the reason for his strength. Samson teased her at first but then revealed the secret, and his head was shaved. After his hair grew out, he killed more Philistines during his death than he did in life. Delilah's fate is never mentioned. Having judged Israel for 20 years, Samson is the last judge recorded in Judges.

The next trek's man of deliberation and woman of honor will be a refreshing change of pace from the hot-tempered Samson and devious Delilah. See you there!

*I have learned to be content whatever the circumstances. I know what it is to be in need, and I know what it is to have plenty. I have learned the secret of being content in any and every situation, whether well fed or hungry, whether living in plenty or in want. I can do all this through him who gives me strength.*
PHILIPPIANS 4:11–13

# BIBLE

# TREK

# VOYAGE 13

## ALIENS

In this voyage you will follow the trek of a woman who grew up surrounded by those who worshipped other gods. In traveling with her mother-in-law back to Israel, she not only abandoned the foreign gods but clung to the beliefs of her mother-in-law. Once in Israel, she worked hard in the fields to feed them both. The story is an enjoyable one with a romantic quality. It is as if the writer is looking back with affection to events in the distant past that have been softened by the filtering effects of time.

### CAPTAIN'S LOG

As we begin this voyage, we wonder what would become of this young widow who moved to a land of people with ways strange to her. Yet she impressed a wealthy landowner with her noble character. With her mother-in-law's guidance, she married again and started a family. The New Testament lists her in the genealogy of the Messiah (Matthew 1:5).

This voyage explores the life of _____ in Moab and her marriage to _____ in Israel.

**1.** Naomi was from what town?

   a. Bethel
   b. Bethlehem
   c. Jerusalem
   d. Nazareth

**2.** Why did Naomi and her family go to Moab?

**3.** Who died first?

   a. Naomi's husband
   b. Naomi's sons

**4.** True or False: Ruth's sister-in-law Orpah was from Judah.

**5.** About how long was Naomi in Moab when both her sons died?

**6.** True or False: Both Ruth and Orpah accompanied Naomi when she left Moab.

**7.** Ruth told Naomi, "Your _____ will be my _____ and your God my God" (same word).

**8.** Naomi said, "I went away _____, but the LORD has brought me back _____.

**9.** Did Naomi have a high or low opinion of Boaz?

**10.** What is *not* true of Boaz's treatment of Ruth?

   a. he invited her to eat with him
   b. he invited Ruth to bring Naomi to gather with her
   c. he said she could drink water from the jars the men had filled
   d. he told the men not to bother her

**11.** What food was Ruth gathering from the land owned by Boaz?

  a. barley and wheat
  b. dates
  c. figs
  d. pomegranates

**12.** Where did Naomi tell Ruth to sleep so Boaz would take notice of her?

**13.** What problem had to be solved before Boaz could marry Ruth?

  a. a closer relative had first choice of the land and Ruth
  b. Boaz did not want to endanger his inheritance by having a child by Ruth
  c. Ruth could not provide the dowry required by Jewish custom
  d. the city elders objected to the marriage

**14.** How did people legalize transactions in Israel at this time?

**15.** True or False: By the time Boaz and Ruth had a son named Obed, Naomi had died.

## BLACK HOLE:

Obed's son was named Jesse, and Jesse's son was named _____.

## VOYAGE 13

■ ■ ■ ■ ■ ■

### ANSWERS

Ruth, Boaz (Ruth 1:4, 22; 4:13)

1. b. Bethlehem (Ruth 1:1–2)
2. because of a famine in Judah (Ruth 1:1)
3. a. Naomi's husband (Ruth 1:3)
4. False—she was from Moab (Ruth 1:4)
5. 10 years (Ruth 1:4)
6. False—only Ruth (Ruth 1:14)
7. "people," "people" (**Ruth 1:16**)
8. "full," "empty" (**Ruth 1:21**)
9. high (Ruth 2:20)
10. b. he invited Ruth to bring Naomi to gather with her (Ruth 2:9, 14)
11. a. barley and wheat (Ruth 2:23)
12. at his feet (Ruth 3:4)
13. a. a closer relative had first choice of the land and Ruth (Ruth 3:12)
14. "one party took off his sandal and gave it to the other" (**Ruth 4:7**)
15. False—Naomi cared for her grandson (Ruth 4:16)

Black Hole: David (Ruth 4:22)

## VOYAGE 13

# WELCOME TO YOUR DEEP SPACE DESTINATION

So how did you do on this voyage? Did you glean a lot of points? Were you amazed by the heroine's steadfastness?

Ruth, a foreigner and widow, and her mother-in-law, Naomi, lived in quiet desperation as Ruth gleaned grain. Boaz, who owned the fields, had heard of her kindness to Naomi. He ensured she would not be molested. Clearly he was interested in her, but how could Ruth be certain?

Every society has unique standards of proper conduct. Ruth, a foreign woman, could easily have run afoul of these customs, but she had Naomi to guide her. Ruth asked Boaz to spread his cloak over her, clearly asking him for protection. It was also Ruth's subtle way of proposing marriage to Boaz.

Ruth's story is a classic with a happy ending. Scores of generations of readers have been deeply affected by it. Ruth's powerful statement "Your people will be my people, and your God my God" is often used in marriage ceremonies today.

*I urge you to live a life worthy*
*of the calling you have received.*
*Be completely humble and gentle;*
*be patient, bearing with one another in love.*
*Make every effort to keep the unity*
*of the Spirit through the bond of peace.*
EPHESIANS 4:1–3

# BIBLE
# TREK

# VOYAGE 14

## RESTORATION AND REMEMBRANCE

Our next trek doesn't follow a person, nor do we challenge a nemesis. Instead, we follow the travels of an extraordinary chest that marked the very presence of God.

This special box was carried by poles that passed through the rings of the container. Apart from touching the poles, humans were forbidden to touch the chest.

### CAPTAIN'S LOG

The chest with the Ten Commandments was carried by the Israelites during their years in the wilderness. Whenever the Israelites camped, they placed the container in the tabernacle, a special tent. The chest accompanied them into the Promised Land but did not always remain in their possession. The chest was captured by their enemies, returned after a time, placed in a temple, and then lost again. In this trek, you'll follow its many travels.

"People will no longer say, 'The ark of the covenant of the LORD.' It will never enter their minds or be remembered; it will not be missed, nor will another one be _____."

**1.** What covered the poles used to carry the ark of the covenant?

**2.** Where were the rings for the poles attached to the ark?

  a. at its four top corners
  b. on its four feet

**3.** How many cherubim were on the top of the ark?

  a. one
  b. two
  c. four
  d. twelve

**4.** True or False: The ark of the covenant was made after the death of Moses.

**5.** "At that time the LORD set apart the tribe of _____ to carry the ark of the covenant of the LORD."

**6.** What enemy were the Israelites fighting when the ark was captured?

   a. the armies of the kings of the Medes
   b. the army of Pharaoh
   c. the army of the king of Babylon
   d. the army of the Philistines

**7.** What was Eli's reaction when he learned his two sons had been killed and the ark captured by the enemy?

**8.** Eli's grandson was named Ichabod, meaning "No glory," as the boy's mother said, "The Glory has _____from Israel."

**9.** The enemy put the stolen ark in the same temple as what false god?

   a. Baal
   b. Dagon
   c. Molech
   d. the goddess Artemis

**10.** The next morning, what had happened to the statue to the false god?

**11.** While the ark was being moved, what caused Uzzah to touch it in an attempt to right it, resulting in his death?

a. a strong east wind blew and upset it
b. oxen pulling the cart carrying it stumbled
c. the men holding it by poles through the rings stumbled
d. Uzzah replaced the lid, which had slipped off

**12.** King David said, "Here I am, living in a _____ of cedar, while the ark of God remains in a tent."

**13.** Who built a temple for the ark?

a. Absalom
b. David
c. Herod the Great
d. Solomon

**14.** When in the tabernacle (tent), the ark was in an area called what?

**15.** According to the book of Hebrews, the ark contained a gold jar of manna, the stone tablets of the covenant, and what third item?

  a. "the bronze snake Moses had put on a pole that the peopled looked at and lived"
  b. "a tribute of gold given by the enemies of Israel when they returned the ark"
  c. "Aaron's staff that had budded"
  d. "the books of the law of Moses"

## BLACK HOLE:

True or False: The high priest could enter the inner room containing the ark only once a year.

## VOYAGE 14

■■■■■■■

## ANSWERS

"made" **(Jeremiah 3:16)**

1. gold (Exodus 25:13)
2. b. on its four feet (Exodus 25:12)
3. b. two (Exodus 25:19)
4. False—he inspected the work after it was built (Exodus 39:43)
5. "Levi" **(Deuteronomy 10:8)**
6. d. the army of the Philistines (1 Samuel 4:10–11)
7. he fell backward off his chair, broke his neck, and died (1 Samuel 4:18)
8. "departed" **(1 Samuel 4:21)**
9. b. Dagon (1 Samuel 5:2)
10. it had fallen on its face before the ark (1 Samuel 5:3)
11. b. oxen pulling the cart carrying it stumbled (2 Samuel 6:6)
12. "house" **(2 Samuel 7:2)**
13. d. Solomon (1 Kings 8:12, 17–21)
14. Most Holy Place (Hebrews 9:2–4)
15. c. "Aaron's staff that had budded" **(Hebrews 9:4)**

Black Hole: True (Hebrews 9:7)

# VOYAGE 14

■■■■■■■

## WELCOME TO YOUR DEEP SPACE DESTINATION

How did you do? These questions ranged through several books of the Bible, so answering them took a thorough knowledge of the events surrounding the travels of the ark.

At first, the ark had no permanent home in the Promised Land. And the Philistines took the ark to several places in their country. At each place misfortune befell them. After possessing the ark for seven months (1 Samuel 6:1), the Philistines wisely returned it to the Israelites. Years passed before David's son Solomon built the temple in Jerusalem to serve as a place to worship and to house the ark.

After the Babylonians destroyed Jerusalem and Solomon's temple, the ark appears to have been lost to the mists of time. In speaking of the ark, the Hebrew writer states, "But we cannot discuss these things in detail now" (Hebrews 9:5). So we now leave this mystery behind and embark upon our next voyage with a lowly shepherd boy.

*In the presence of God and of Christ Jesus,*
*who will judge the living and the dead,*
*and in view of his appearing and his kingdom,*
*I give you this charge: Preach the word;*
*be prepared in season and out of season;*
*correct, rebuke and encourage—*
*with great patience and careful instruction.*
2 TIMOTHY 4:1–2

# BIBLE

# TREK

# VOYAGE 15

■ ■ ■ ■ ■ ■ ■

## "THE HARDER THEY FALL"

All through the reign of Saul—Israel's first king—the Philistines threatened Israel. In this Bible trek, Saul's army and the Philistines faced each other across a deep valley. Whoever charged first would have to descend into the valley and be at a distinct disadvantage. During the stalemate, a seemingly invincible Philistine giant stood on the hillside and taunted the Israelites to a one-on-one contest. Not even King Saul, the tallest man in Israel, would accept the challenge. To learn what happened next, read the Captain's Log.

### CAPTAIN'S LOG

A young shepherd boy who had come to deliver food to his brothers was astonished that no one accepted the giant's challenge. Armed only with a staff, stones, and a sling, the young boy faced the giant. The confrontation became one of the most famous stories in the Bible.

The names of the shepherd boy and the giant have become part of an expression for an unequally matched contest, known as a _____ and _____ battle.

**1.** Which prophet told Saul his kingdom would be taken away?

**2.** "To obey is _____ than sacrifice, and to heed is _____ than the fat of rams" (same word).

**3.** What was the name of David's father?

**4.** "People look at the outward appearance, but the LORD looks at the _____."

**5.** True or False: David was the youngest son in his family.

**6.** What instrument did David play to soothe Saul's troubled mind?

**7.** How many days did Goliath taunt the Israelites to send a man to fight him?

    a. 7
    b. 12
    c. 40
    d. a full year

**8.** What did Saul promise to a warrior who defeated Goliath?

    a. great wealth
    b. his daughter in matrimony
    c. exemption of his family from taxes
    d. all of the above

**9.** In addition to a lion, what other animal did David kill while keeping sheep?

    a. a "great beast"
    b. a bear
    c. a wolf
    d. an eagle

**10.** How many smooth stones did David select from the stream?

**11.** True or False: The only weapon Goliath carried was a spear.

**12.** Where did the stone from David's sling strike Goliath?

**13.** Whose weapon did David use to sever Goliath's head?

a. a knife belonging to Goliath's armor bearer
b. Goliath's own sword
c. a sword belonging to David's older brother
d. a sword given to him by Saul

**14.** "Saul has slain his _____, and David his tens of _____" (same word).

**15.** What was Jonathan's relationship to David?

    a. David's chief rival in Saul's court
    b. David's best friend

# BLACK HOLE:

What was the name of Saul's daughter whom David married?

## VOYAGE 15

■ ■ ■ ■ ■ ■

### ANSWERS

David, Goliath (1 Samuel 17:4, 32)

1. Samuel (1 Samuel 15:26)
2. "better," "better" **(1 Samuel 15:22)**
3. Jesse (1 Samuel 17:13–14)
4. "heart" **(1 Samuel 16:7)**
5. True (1 Samuel 17:13–14)
6. lyre or harp (1 Samuel 16:16)
7. c. 40 days (1 Samuel 17:16)
8. d. all of the above (1 Samuel 17:25)
9. b. a bear (1 Samuel 17:36)
10. five (1 Samuel 17:40)
11. False—he carried sword, spear, and javelin (1 Samuel 17:45)
12. forehead (1 Samuel 17:49)
13. b. Goliath's own sword (1 Samuel 17:51)
14. "thousands," "thousands" **(1 Samuel 18:7)**
15. b. David's best friend (1 Samuel 19:1)

Black Hole: Michal (1 Samuel 18:27)

# VOYAGE 15

## WELCOME TO YOUR DEEP SPACE DESTINATION

So, did you walk away from this voyage in victory (like David) or defeat (like Goliath)? Seemingly invincible in his heavy body armor, Goliath did not seem too concerned with the teenage shepherd boy. But his armor did not protect his forehead, and the stone from David's sling struck him there.

Saul had tried to dissuade David from going into battle. He said, "You are not able to go out against this Philistine and fight him; you are only a young man, and he has been a warrior from his youth" (1 Samuel 17:33). But David believed the Lord who had rescued him from the lion and the bear would rescue him from the sword of the Philistine. While others saw a well-armored giant, David saw a mortal man defying an all-powerful God.

During each person's life, giants must be faced. They can be daunting and appear insurmountable. Take courage in the face of fearful circumstances. Face the giant with the full armor of God.

*Stand firm then,*
*with the belt of truth buckled around your waist,*
*with the breastplate of righteousness in place,*
*and with your feet fitted with the readiness*
*that comes from the gospel of peace.*
EPHESIANS 6:14–15

# BIBLE TREK

# VOYAGE 16

## DUEL IN THE SUN

Welcome to your next voyage where, once again, a king who did not follow the commands of God ruled the people of Israel. Ahab, who was not a pleasant individual to begin with, married the domineering Jezebel, who enhanced his evil ways and employed a few of her own. Jezebel wanted not merely to pursue the worship of Baal and Asherah but also labored to establish such worship throughout Israel. Ahab built an altar to Baal and set up Asherah poles. Countering the idol worship were the prophets of God, who were being hunted down and killed. Most fled to caves and mountains.

### CAPTAIN'S LOG

In this voyage you will see a prophet of God who, when facing several hundred prophets of Baal in a duel on a mountaintop, claimed the true God would be the one who answered by fire. The people of Israel were fortunate to have such a strong prophet as their leader.

The prophet of God who overcame the prophets of Baal on the mountaintop was _____.

**1.** Based on where he was from, Elijah the prophet was also known as Elijah the
_____.

 **2.** What disaster did Elijah tell Ahab would come on the land of Israel?

a. a dust storm would hide the sun for 40 days
b. foreign invaders would lay waste of his kingdom
c. hail would destroy crops and kill cattle
d. the land would have neither rain nor dew

 **3.** What type of birds fed Elijah while he hid in the Kerith Ravine?

 **4.** True or False: The widow of Zarephath, the town where Elijah stayed, had two daughters and seven sons.

**5.** What was the widow doing when Elijah came to her house?

    a. gathering sticks
    b. making clothes for a neighboring woman
    c. preparing to kill her last goat
    d. singing psalms and hymns

**6.** "For the jar of _____ was not used up and the jug of _____ did not run dry" (two words).

**7.** What other miracle happened while Elijah was with the widow?

**8.** When Ahab saw Elijah, he said, "Is that you, you _____ of Israel?"

**9.** How can Obadiah, Ahab's administrator, be described?

    a. an evil man who set up an altar for Baal
    b. a committed believer in God

**10.** True or False: Elijah was the only one in Israel who had not bowed down to Baal.

**11.** On what mount did Elijah have the challenge with the prophets of Baal?

**12.** How many prophets of Baal were on the mountain?

    a. 12
    b. 40
    c. 77
    d. 450

**13.** What did the prophets of Baal do to get the attention of their god?

    a. cut themselves
    b. danced
    c. shouted
    d. all of the above

**14.** How did Elijah's servant describe the rain cloud rising from the sea?

**15.** How did the Lord speak to Elijah after he fled from Jezebel's threat to kill him within 24 hours?

    a. in a fire
    b. in a gentle whisper
    c. in a powerful wind
    d. in an earthquake

# BLACK HOLE:

What was the name of the prophet who received Elijah's cloak?

## VOYAGE 16

### ANSWERS

Elijah (1 Kings 18:18–19)

1. Tishbite (1 Kings 17:1)
2. d. the land would have neither rain nor dew (1 Kings 17:1)
3. ravens (1 Kings 17:5–6)
4. False—only one son (1 Kings 17:12)
5. a. gathering sticks (1 Kings 17:10)
6. "flour," "oil" (**1 Kings 17:16**)
7. her son was raised from the dead (1 Kings 17:22–23)
8. "troubler" (**1 Kings 18:17**)
9. b. a committed believer in God (1 Kings 18:3)
10. False—7,000 had not bowed (1 Kings 19:18)
11. Carmel (1 Kings 18:20)
12. d. 450 (1 Kings 18:19, 22)
13. d. all of the above (1 Kings 18:26–28)
14. "as small as a man's hand" (**1 Kings 18:44**)
15. b. in a gentle whisper (1 Kings 19:11–13)

Black Hole: Elisha (1 Kings 19:19)

## VOYAGE 18

# WELCOME TO YOUR DEEP SPACE DESTINATION

Congratulations! You have passed the midpoint of your Bible trek. Have you found that your skill at answering the questions is growing as you progress?

Until God set him straight, Elijah believed that he was the only one who had not worshipped Baal. One can understand how he might have believed so. Obadiah, Ahab's chief servant, had secretly hidden God's prophets and supplied them with food. For three years, Elijah himself had been in hiding. But he met with Ahab to propose a direct contest between God and Baal and to foretell the end of the drought. During the mountaintop duel, the Baal prophets' noisy dancing, shouting, and cutting of themselves to arouse their god was an interesting contrast to Elijah's cool confidence as the people soaked his altar with water and he prayed a simple prayer.

*Therefore confess your sins to each other*
*and pray for each other so that you may be healed.*
*The prayer of a righteous person is powerful and effective.*
*Elijah was a human being, even as we are.*
*He prayed earnestly that it would not rain,*
*and it did not rain on the land for three and a half years.*
*Again he prayed, and the heavens gave rain,*
*and the earth produced its crops.*
JAMES 5:16–18

# BIBLE
# TREK

# VOYAGE 17

## UNINTENDED CONSEQUENCES

Go now on a Bible trek that is one of the most suspenseful stories in the Bible. It has all the ingredients to make it a classic: a powerful king, a beautiful queen, a man of ordinary means, and a vain and pretentious chief official. The final conflict ends with one of the best-known reversals of fortune in history.

King Xerxes ruled the vast Persian Empire. It extended from Ethiopia in Africa to India in the Far East. Although he possessed great power and riches, a personal weakness—a temper that could explode in fury—also plagued him.

### CAPTAIN'S LOG

On this voyage you must navigate through dangerous political intrigue. The story begins with a special banquet for the nobles and officials of the 127 provinces in the Persian Empire. After they enjoyed the splendor and fine food of his great banquet, King Xerxes sent for a beautiful "possession" for them to admire.

Two books of the Old Testament are named for women: Ruth and _____.

**1.** Why did Queen Vashti lose favor with King Xerxes?

**2.** True or False: In deciding what to do about Queen Vashti, King Xerxes consulted priests of Baal.

**3.** What was Mordecai's relationship to Esther?

a. brother
b. uncle
c. cousin
d. no relation except he was from the same clan

**4.** True or False: At first, Mordecai told Esther *not* to reveal that she was Jewish.

**5.** How many months did Esther undergo beauty treatments before being presented to King Xerxes?

**6.** Who received credit for uncovering the plot against King Xerxes?

    a. Haman
    b. Hegai, the one in charge of the harem
    c. Mordecai
    d. Queen Esther

**7.** Why did Haman become enraged at Mordecai?

**8.** Haman's decree was to kill all the Jews during what period of time?

    a. secretly over seven years
    b. publicly all on the same day

**9.** When Mordecai learned of Haman's decree, he tore his clothes and put on _____ and ashes.

**10.** When Queen Esther came unannounced to see King Xerxes, she would be killed unless the king did what?

**11.** Esther said, "I will go to the king, even though it is against the law. And if I _____, I _____" (same word).

**12.** Other than King Xerxes, who else did Queen Esther invite to the banquets that she prepared?

   a. Haman and his wife Zeresh
   b. Haman only
   c. her maids in waiting
   d. Mordecai

**13.** What caused King Xerxes to have the book of chronicles of his reign read to him?

   a. it was a yearly ritual started by his wise advisers
   b. Haman requested it
   c. he could not sleep
   d. he was bothered by a question from Queen Esther

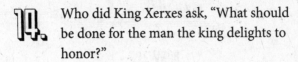

**14.** Who did King Xerxes ask, "What should be done for the man the king delights to honor?"

**15.** After Queen Esther identified Haman as her enemy to King Xerxes, what did Haman do that enraged King Xerxes still further?

    a. tried to escape by entering the women's court

    b. appealed to Esther and fell on her couch

    c. asked palace guards to hide him

    d. used the king's signet ring to forge a document refuting Esther's claim

# BLACK HOLE:

What Jewish observance began as the result of their escape from death?

## VOYAGE 17

■ ■ ■ ■ ■ ■ ■

### ANSWERS

#### Esther

1. she refused to come when Xerxes sent for her (Esther 1:12)
2. False—he consulted his wise men (Esther 1:13)
3. c. cousin, who raised the orphaned Esther (Esther 2:7)
4. True (Esther 2:10)
5. 12 (Esther 2:12)
6. c. Mordecai (Esther 2:21–22)
7. Mordecai would neither kneel down nor pay honor to Haman (Esther 3:5)
8. b. publicly all on the same day (Esther 3:13)
9. sackcloth (Esther 4:1)
10. extended his gold scepter to her (Esther 4:11)
11. "perish," "perish" **(Esther 4:16)**
12. b. Haman only (Esther 5:4, 7)
13. c. he could not sleep (Esther 6:1)
14. Haman **(Esther 6:6)**
15. b. appealed to Esther and fell on her couch (Esther 7:8)

Black Hole: Purim (Esther 9:26–27)

# VOYAGE 17

██ ██ ██ ██ ██ ██ ██

## WELCOME TO YOUR DEEP SPACE DESTINATION

Did you bravely find your way through this sea of questions? Or did a tempest blow you off course?

Queen Esther successfully navigated through dangerous political intrigue to save her people. After a dark moment when it appeared the Jews would be killed and Mordecai executed, Haman's plans took an unexpected turn. He became the one executed, and Mordecai was raised in his place.

Mordecai encouraged the people of God to have a special feast of thanksgiving for their triumph over their enemies. The Jews kept the feast every year after that, and the feast of Purim is still celebrated today.

During your next trek, you'll be doing some time traveling. So set your watches and let's go!

*Rejoice in the Lord always. I will say it again: Rejoice! Let your gentleness be evident to all. The Lord is near. Do not be anxious about anything, but in every situation, by prayer and petition, with thanksgiving, present your requests to God. And the peace of God, which transcends all understanding, will guard your hearts and your minds in Christ Jesus.*
PHILIPPIANS 4:4–7

# BIBLE
# TREK

# VOYAGE 18

■ ■ ■ ■ ■ ■ ■

## QUANTUM LEAP

■ ■ ■ ■

How have you done so far? Some of the treks are limited in time and scope. Others range throughout the Bible. The next trek takes you into strange new territory—into the minds of prophets who lived in the past but saw into the future. Their amazing visions display the majesty and glory of God. Check the Captain's Log carefully, because knowing these prophets and their visions will make answering the questions easier.

### CAPTAIN'S LOG

Three visionaries come into view. Two of them were with people of Jerusalem who had been taken captive and made the 900-mile trek to Babylon. The third lived in isolation on a small, rocky island. The first two lived in Old Testament times; the third one's vision is recorded in the last book of the New Testament.

The three prophets are Ezekiel on the Kebar River, _____ who interpreted a dream of King Nebuchadnezzar of Babylon, and _____ on the island of Patmos.

**1.** How many living creatures did Ezekiel see in his vision?

**2.** Each of the living creatures had faces of a human being, a lion, an ox, and an

_____.

**3.** True or False: Each of the living creatures had wings.

**4.** Throughout the book of Ezekiel, the prophet is addressed by the Lord as "_____ of man."

**5.** What was Ezekiel told to do with the scroll filled with lament, mourning, and woe?

    a. burn it and scatter the ashes
    b. bury it for forty days
    c. eat it
    d. read it to the people of Israel

**6.** How was Ezekiel to serve the people of Israel?

    a. as a bearer of light
    b. as a voice calling in the wilderness
    c. as a high priest
    d. as a watchman

**7.** While in exile, Ezekiel made a model of and laid siege works against what city?

**8.** In the valley showed to him by the Lord, as Ezekiel prophesied, what happened to cause the rattling sound?

**9.** True or False: Daniel and the three other young men with him looked healthy because Nebuchadnezzar's chief official provided them royal food.

**10.** Why were Nebuchadnezzar's astrologers unable to give an interpretation of his dream?

    a. Daniel told them to remain silent
    b. Nebuchadnezzar would not tell them the contents of the dream
    c. They feared telling Nebuchadnezzar that his kingdom would crumble
    d. Nebuchadnezzar's rivals threatened them

**11.** Daniel said the statue in Nebuchadnezzar's dream represented how many kingdoms?

**12.** How did the words "MENE, MENE, TEKEL, PARSIN" come to appear on the plaster wall of King Belshazzar's palace?

**13.** In Revelation, the Lord God told John, "I am the Alpha and the _____."

**14.** In Revelation, which of the four horses is the one whose rider represents death?

    a. black horse
    b. fiery, red horse
    c. pale horse
    d. white horse

**15.** True or False: The scroll that John was told to eat tasted as sweet as honey in his mouth.

# BLACK HOLE:

What is the name of the city that is described in Revelation as "Fallen! Fallen is _____ the Great!" and "The merchants of the earth grew rich from her excessive luxuries."

# VOYAGE 18

■ ■ ■ ■ ■ ■

## ANSWERS

Daniel, John (Daniel 1:1–6; 2:24; Revelation 1:9)

1. four (Ezekiel 1:5)
2. eagle (Ezekiel 1:10)
3. True (Ezekiel 1:6)
4. "son" (**Ezekiel 2:3**, and elsewhere)
5. c. eat it (Ezekiel 2:10–3:1)
6. d. as a watchman (Ezekiel 3:17)
7. Jerusalem (Ezekiel 4:1–2)
8. dry bones coming together (Ezekiel 37:4–7)
9. False—they refused to eat what the king provided (Daniel 1:12–15)
10. b. Nebuchadnezzar would not tell them the contents of the dream (Daniel 2:1–9)
11. four (Daniel 2:30–31, 40)
12. they were written by the fingers of a human hand that came out of nowhere (**Daniel 5:**5, **25**)
13. "Omega" (**Revelation 1:8**)
14. c. pale horse (Revelation 6:8)
15. True (Revelation 10:10)

Black Hole: "Babylon" (**Revelation 18:2–3**)

# VOYAGE 18

## WELCOME TO YOUR DEEP SPACE DESTINATION

Did you realize your visions of grandeur on this voyage, or did your score end up to be a pitiful sight?

Ezekiel's vision of the wheels within wheels is one of the best-known visions in the Bible. His first vision was not his only one. He was also commanded by God to act out the events that were about to befall Jerusalem, including building a model of the city and showing that it would eventually fall because of the people's sins.

Daniel, like Ezekiel, had been taken to Babylon. Daniel not only told King Nebuchadnezzar the contents of the dream but also interpreted it. The end of his interpretation was that all the earthly kingdoms would be crushed by God's kingdom, one that would endure forever.

John's vision is a rich one filled with vivid imagery that is almost beyond human understanding. But one of the key elements is that the force of God and good will prevail over the force of Satan and evil.

*Dear friend,*
*do not imitate what is evil but what is good.*
*Anyone who does what is good is from God.*
*Anyone who does what is evil*
*has not seen God.*

3 JOHN 1:11

# BIBLE

# TREK

# VOYAGE 19

■ ■ ■ ■ ■ ■ ■

## AWOL

Has a lack of confidence or certainty ever led you to try to shirk the task God asked you to tackle? You're not alone. The Bible recounts many occasions when the Lord gave special missions to certain individuals, only to have them try to avoid the assignment. Moses tried to excuse himself from representing God before Pharaoh by claiming to be a poor speaker. Gideon requested verification of God's call with a fleece. In this trek, we follow the adventures of one of the most reluctant Old Testament prophets.

### CAPTAIN'S LOG

God called the prophet of this Bible trek to preach to Israel's enemy—the sinful city of Nineveh, the capital of Assyria. Instead, the prophet tried to avoid his assignment by going AWOL—absent without leave. Rather than repentance and salvation, the prophet preferred to see the city get hammered by God's wrath. He set out for Tarshish, which was in the opposite direction from Nineveh and all the way across the Mediterranean Sea.

The prophet who went AWOL was _____.

**1.** Why did Jonah take a ship bound for Tarshish?

**2.** From what city did Jonah find a ship bound for Tarshish?

**3.** During the storm, as the sailors threw cargo from the ship to lighten it, what was Jonah doing?

  a. praying
  b. sleeping

**4.** Who identified Jonah as the one who caused the storm to strike the ship?

  a. a prophet of a false god
  b. an angel of the Lord
  c. Jonah himself
  d. the sailors by casting lots

**5.** Who suggested that throwing Jonah in the sea would stop the great storm?

    a. an angel of the Lord
    b. Jonah himself
    c. the captain of the ship
    d. the seamen

**6.** True or False: At first the seamen were reluctant to throw Jonah overboard and tried to row to shore.

**7.** "Those who cling to worthless _____ turn away from God's love for them."

**8.** How many days did it take to walk through the city of Nineveh?

**9.** Jonah warned that Nineveh would be overthrown in how many days?

**10.** True or False: The people of Nineveh gave up their evil ways and put on sackcloth and prayed, but the king issued a decree telling his nobles to ignore the preaching of Jonah.

**11.** Jonah said, "I knew that you are a gracious and _____ God, slow to anger and abounding in love."

**12.** What killed the leafy plant that gave Jonah shade?

a. a hot east wind
b. a worm provided by God
c. roots without depth
d. the scorching sun

**13.** What was Jonah more concerned about than the city of Nineveh?

**14.** After Nineveh was spared, Jonah said he was so _____ he wished he were dead.

**15.** Who said, "The men of Nineveh will stand up at the judgment with this generation and condemn it"?

# BLACK HOLE:

What part of their body did the Lord use metaphorically to describe how the people of Nineveh were lost?

## VOYAGE 19

■ ■ ■ ■ ■ ■ ■

### ANSWERS

Jonah (Jonah 1:1–3)

1. to run away from the Lord (Jonah 1:3)
2. Joppa (Jonah 1:3)
3. b. sleeping (Jonah 1:4–6)
4. d. the sailors by casting lots (Jonah 1:7)
5. b. Jonah himself (Jonah 1:12)
6. True (Jonah 1:13)
7. "idols" (**Jonah 2:8**)
8. three (Jonah 3:3)
9. 40 (Jonah 3:4)
10. False—the king's decree also called for repentance (Jonah 3:7–9)
11. "compassionate" (**Jonah 4:2**)
12. b. a worm provided by God (Jonah 4:7)
13. a plant that had provided him shade (Jonah 4:10–11)
14. angry (Jonah 4:9)
15. Jesus (**Luke 11:**29, **32**)

Black Hole: hand—"people who cannot tell their right hand from their left" (**Jonah 4:11**)

# VOYAGE 19

## WELCOME TO YOUR DEEP SPACE DESTINATION

How well did you do? Although the book of Jonah is short, only four chapters, it's important because it compels us to examine our own lives. As we see Jonah try to flee from God, we see ourselves out of the corner of our eye and wonder if we are fully following the plan that God has for us. Only by prayer and study of God's word can we come to understand His will for us.

Jonah found it repugnant to preach to the people of Nineveh. His fear was not that they wouldn't repent. He feared they would. Amazingly enough, Jonah did not want to see Nineveh be given the same compassion from God that he himself had received.

Nineveh was the center of pagan worship in the region. Despite this, its citizens were precious to God even if they did not know Him. The book of Jonah is a clear expression of God's love and compassion for all life—men, women, children, and animals as well.

*Here is a trustworthy saying that deserves full acceptance:*
*Christ Jesus came into the world to save sinners—*
*of whom I am the worst. But for that very reason*
*I was shown mercy so that in me, the worst of sinners,*
*Christ Jesus might display his immense patience*
*as an example for those who would believe in him*
*and receive eternal life.*
1 TIMOTHY 1:15–16

# BIBLE
# TREK

# VOYAGE 20

## CONSCIENCE AND THE KING

So how did you fare in the previous voyages that were centered on the Old Testament? Ready to test your knowledge of the New Testament?

The central theme of the Old Testament was the promise that God was going to bless the world, not merely the Jews. And He would do so through the lineage of King David. But what form would the reign of this promised sovereign take, and when would he come? The following Captain's Log tells about a prophet who wasn't the Messiah but prepared the way for him.

### CAPTAIN'S LOG

The Gospels of Matthew, Mark, Luke, and John all introduced a prophet who announced the coming of the Messiah. All four Gospels quote Isaiah 40:3 in describing the prophet as one who would "Prepare the way for the LORD." This individual also faced a nemesis who would eventually behead him. So put your thinking cap on and let's begin!

The Bible verse "I will send my messenger ahead of you, who will prepare your way," refers to _____ the _____ (two words).

1.  Isaiah wrote, "A voice of one calling: 'In the _____ prepare the way for the LORD.'"

2.  What was the name of the angel who announced John the Baptist's birth to his father?

    a. Gabriel
    b. Michael

3.  Because of his unbelief, what condition struck Zechariah until the time his son, John the Baptist, was named?

4.  Who was the caesar when John the Baptist began preaching?

    a. Caligula
    b. Claudius
    c. Nero
    d. Tiberius

**5.** John the Baptist told soldiers, "Don't extort money and don't accuse people falsely—be content with your _____."

**6.** John said he baptized with water, but the one who came after would baptize with the _____ _____ (two words).

**7.** According to the Gospel of John, what expression did John the Baptist use to describe Jesus?

    a. "Everlasting Rabbi"
    b. "Lamb of God"
    c. "Son of Man"
    d. "Word with God"

**8.** What expression did John the Baptist use to describe the Pharisees and Sadducees?

    a. "brood of vipers"
    b. "children of the Most High"
    c. "sons of Beelzebul"
    d. "leaders with uncircumcised hearts"

**9.** According to Jesus, who is greater than John the Baptist?

**10.** True or False: Herod the tetrarch believed Jesus was John the Baptist raised from the dead.

**11.** What was the name of the woman whom John the Baptist said was not lawful for Herod to have?

**12.** How was the woman's husband, Philip, related to Herod?

**13.** At first, why did Herod not have John the Baptist killed?

    a.  Herod feared John the Baptist would come back to life

    b.  Herod feared the people

    c.  it pleased Herod to make sport of John the Baptist at his royal banquets

    d.  the high priest warned Herod not to kill a holy man

**14.** What event was Herod celebrating when John the Baptist was beheaded?

**15.** True or False: After his death, Herod had John the Baptist's body burned.

# BLACK HOLE:

In the Gospel of Matthew, Jesus compares John the Baptist to which Old Testament prophet.

# VOYAGE 20

■■■■■■■

## ANSWERS

John, Baptist (**Mark 1:2**, 4)

1. "wilderness" (**Isaiah 40:3**)
2. a. Gabriel (Luke 1:19)
3. he could not speak (Luke 1:13, 20)
4. d. Tiberius (Luke 3:1–3)
5. "pay" (**Luke 3:14**)
6. Holy Spirit (Mark 1:8)
7. b. "Lamb of God" (**John 1:29**)
8. a. "brood of vipers" (**Matthew 3:7**)
9. "whoever is least in the kingdom of heaven" (**Matthew 11:11**)
10. True (Matthew 14:1–2)
11. Herodias (Matthew 14:3–4)
12. Philip was Herod's brother (John 14:3–4)
13. b. Herod feared the people (Matthew 14:5)
14. Herod's birthday (Matthew 14:6)
15. False—the disciples buried the body (Matthew 14:12)

Black Hole: Elijah (Matthew 11:13–14)

# VOYAGE 20

■■■■■■■

## WELCOME TO YOUR DEEP SPACE DESTINATION

How did you do this time around? Were those questions a royal pain to answer?

The Herod family of royals was a large and complicated one, because Herod the Great had several wives and sons. After his death, one son, Herod Antipas, ruled over Galilee. Another son named Philip married Herodias, who was the daughter of still another of Herod the Great's sons. So her husband, Philip, was also her half uncle. But Herodias left Philip to marry Herod Antipas—he was one of her half uncles, too.

John the Baptist preached against the marriage of Herod and Herodias. Herod solved the problem by putting John in a dungeon. Then, with the help of her daughter, Herodias managed to maneuver her husband into the rash vow that resulted in the death of John the Baptist. And so passed the man of whom Jesus said, "Among those born of women there has not risen anyone greater than John the Baptist" (Matthew 11:11).

> "Look, the Lamb of God,
> who takes away the sin of the world!
> This is the one I meant when I said,
> 'A man who comes after me has surpassed me
> because he was before me.'"
> JOHN 1:29–30

# BIBLE

# TREK

# VOYAGE 21

## STAR CHILD

Congratulations on finishing the first of the New Testament Bible treks. Are you traveling at Maximum Warp Speed, or did you get caught in a Tractor Beam? Regardless of your previous triumphs or disappointments, get ready for your next adventure. It's a new type of trek—one you haven't experienced before. You fall into a Temporal Discontinuity.

### CAPTAIN'S LOG

A *Temporal Discontinuity* is a sudden jump in time. This voyage jumps from a prophecy in the Old Testament to its fulfillment in the New. Many Old Testament prophecies remained a mystery until the writers of the New Testament revealed their meanings. More than 40 Old Testament verses are linked directly with the baby born in this trek—a Star Child that wise men and women still seek today. Micah prophesied the place of His birth (Micah 5:2–4). So let's jump right in!

"But you, _____, in the land of Judah. . . out of you will come a ruler who will shepherd my people Israel."

**1.** Matthew's genealogy of Jesus begins with which most ancient individual?

    a. Abraham
    b. Adam
    c. David
    d. Moses

**2.** Each group of Matthew's genealogy of Jesus has how many generations?

**3.** True or False: Luke's genealogy of Jesus traces Jesus' ancestors back to Adam.

**4.** At the time the angels announced that Mary would have the child to be named Jesus, she and Joseph were living in the town of _____.

**5.** Mary accepted what the angel said to her by saying, "I am the Lord's _____."

**6.** True or False: Mary lived in the region of Judea, but Elizabeth lived in Samaria.

**7.** Which caesar authorized the census that caused Joseph and Mary to travel to the "town of David" (Luke 2:4)?

  a. Augustus
  b. Claudius
  c. Nero
  d. Tiberius

**8.** What was the first thing the angel said to the shepherds?

  a. "a light has been born for the Gentiles"
  b. "a Savior has been born"
  c. "do not be afraid"
  d. "I bring you good news"

**9.** The heavenly host sang, "Glory to God in the highest heaven, and on earth _____ to those on whom his favor rests."

**10.** Who did King Herod consult to learn where the king of the Jews would be born?

    a. "chief priests and teachers of the law"
    b. John the Baptist
    c. "soothsayers"
    d. "the magi" (wise men)

**11.** What metal did the magi give to Jesus?

**12.** Where did Jesus' parents flee with Him when Herod ordered the killing of all boys two years old and younger in and around Bethlehem?

**13.** Herod's slaughter of the innocents is described in Jeremiah with the words, "A voice is heard in Ramah. . . _____ weeping for her children."

**14.** What reason did the angel give to Joseph that it was safe to return home?

**15.** When Jesus was first presented at the temple, the two people who recognized Him as the Lord's Messiah were named Simeon and _____.

# BLACK HOLE:

How old was Jesus when He made the statement that He must be in His Father's house (or about His Father's business)?

# VOYAGE 21

## ANSWERS

"Bethlehem" **(Matthew 2:6)**

1. a. Abraham (Matthew 1:2)
2. 14 (Matthew 1:17)
3. True (Luke 3:38)
4. Nazareth (Luke 1:26–27)
5. "servant" **(Luke 1:38)**
6. False—Mary lived in Galilee, Elizabeth in Judea (Luke 1:26, 39)
7. a. Augustus **(Luke 2:1, 4)**
8. c. "do not be afraid" **(Luke 2:10)**
9. "peace" **(Luke 2:14)**
10. a. "chief priests and teachers of the law" **(Matthew 2:4)**
11. gold (Matthew 2:11)
12. Egypt (Matthew 2:13–16)
13. "Rachel" **(Jeremiah 31:15; Matthew 2:17)**
14. those trying to kill the child were dead (Matthew 2:19–20)
15. Anna (Luke 2:25–38)

Black Hole: 12 years old (Luke 2:42, 49)

# VOYAGE 21

## WELCOME TO YOUR DEEP SPACE DESTINATION

Congratulations! You've completed the first of the Temporal Dislocations. There will be more of the Old Testament to New Testament jumps as you trek through the life of Jesus.

Stargazers of ancient times had remarkable ability to plot the course of the planets and to identify stellar arrangements. They knew the night sky so well that any celestial event, no matter how minor, would come to their attention. It might be the slightest change in the brightness of a star, the appearance of a new star, or two planets passing close together. The star of Bethlehem may have been barely discernible or vividly spectacular. But the star was merely a sign. The magi came to worship the one to whom the sign pointed—Jesus Christ, the Savior of the world. Now that this trek is over, let's take a leap of faith into the next!

> "I, Jesus, have sent my angel
> to give you this testimony for the churches.
> I am the Root and the Offspring of David,
> and the bright Morning Star."
> The Spirit and the bride say, "Come!"
> And let the one who hears say, "Come!"
> Let the one who is thirsty come;
> and let the one who wishes take the free gift
> of the water of life.
> REVELATION 22:16–17

# BIBLE
# TREK

# VOYAGE 22

## FUTURE PERFECT

The baby Jesus survived Herod's determined efforts to destroy a rival king. Unknown to Herod and to many others was the nature of the kingdom Jesus would establish. In this Bible trek you will once again begin with verses from the Old Testament and jump to the New Testament to see how His nature was more perfectly revealed.

### CAPTAIN'S LOG

Following His appearance at the Temple when He was 12 years old, the Bible is silent about Jesus until His public ministry began. At that point, His listeners questioned who He was and what He intended to do. Was He an Old Testament prophet raised from the dead? Was He a ruler like David who would triumph in physical battle over Israel's enemies? The name used in the scripture below revealed His true nature—to people of the past, those of the present, and future generations.

"Therefore the Lord himself will give you a sign: The virgin will conceive and give birth to a son, and will call him _____."

**1.** What does Immanuel mean?

**2.** "For to us a child is born, to us a son is given, and the government will be on his shoulders. And he will be called Wonderful _____, Mighty God, Everlasting Father, Prince of _____" (two words).

**3.** "The people walking in _____ have seen a great _____; on those living in the land of deep _____ a _____ has dawned" (two words, each repeated).

**4.** "You are a priest forever, in the order of _____."

**5.** John the Baptist would know that Jesus was God's Chosen One if the Spirit came down as a what?

    a. dove
    b. tongue of fire

**6.** True or False: John the Baptist said he was not the Messiah, but "the voice of one calling in the wilderness, 'Make straight the way for the Lord.'"

**7.** Who went to Simon Peter and said he had found the Messiah?

**8.** How did Peter answer Jesus' question, "Who do you say I am?"

a. "You are Jeremiah or one of the prophets"
b. "You are one born out of due season"
c. "You are the Messiah"
d. "You are the Son of Man"

**9.** Before God said to listen to Jesus on the Mount of Transfiguration, how many shelters did Peter propose to put up?

**10.** What kind of jar contained the perfume that the woman poured on the head of Jesus at the home of Simon the Leper?

**11.** In what city did Jesus arrive on a donkey's colt?

**12.** Who in the Old Testament prophesied that Jesus would come victorious seated on a donkey's colt?

a. Daniel
b. Isaiah
c. Jeremiah
d. Zechariah

**13.** True or False: When the Pharisees told Jesus to rebuke His disciples for their praise of Him, Jesus said that if they kept quiet a legion of angels would descend.

**14.** To whom did Jesus say that His kingdom was not of this world?

a. John the Baptist, as Jesus was being baptized
b. Mary Magdalene, after Jesus rose from the dead
c. Peter, as he left the boat to walk on the water
d. the Roman governor Pilate, as Jesus was brought before him

**15.** "_____, _____, you who kill the prophets and stone those sent to you, how often I have longed to gather your children together, as a hen gathers her chicks under her wings, and you were not willing" (same word—name of city).

## BLACK HOLE:

Jesus revealed himself as the Messiah to what woman who said, "I know that Messiah" (called Christ) "is coming. When he comes, he will explain everything to us."

a. Mary, who sat at the Lord's feet, listening to Him

b. the woman at the well in Samaria

c. the woman who anointed Him with costly perfume

d. the woman who said to herself, "If I only touch his cloak, I will be healed"

## VOYAGE 22

### ANSWERS

"Immanuel" **(Isaiah 7:14)**

1. "God with us" **(Matthew 1:23)**
2. "Counselor," "Peace" **(Isaiah 9:6)**
3. "darkness," "light," "darkness," "light" **(Isaiah 9:2)**
4. "Melchizedek" **(Psalm 110:4)**
5. a. dove (John 1:32–34)
6. True **(John 1:23)**
7. Andrew, Peter's brother (John 1:40–42)
8. c. "You are the Messiah" **(Matthew 16:16)**
9. three—one each for Jesus, Moses, and Elijah (Matthew 17:4)
10. alabaster (Matthew 26:6–7)
11. Jerusalem (John 12:12–15)
12. d. Zechariah (Zechariah 9:9)
13. False—He said the stones would cry out (Luke 19:39–40)
14. d. the Roman governor Pilate, as Jesus was brought before him (John 18:35–36)
15. "Jerusalem," "Jerusalem" **(Luke 13:34)**

Black Hole: b. the woman at the well in Samaria **(John 4:25)**

# VOYAGE 22

## WELCOME TO YOUR DEEP SPACE DESTINATION

Who is Jesus? On the Mount of Transfiguration, God explained, "This is my Son, whom I love; with him I am well pleased. Listen to him!" (Matthew 17:5). He was the Son of God. His ministry was a unique one. He often spoke to a limited number of disciples, yet He preached to vast multitudes. He presented sermons of grand spiritual visions, yet He could reveal simple truths by talking about events in the everyday lives of His humble listeners.

Have you been enjoying your treks to interesting locations, following the battles of good versus evil, and the Temporal Jumps from Old Testament to New Testament? At times you may have found the Bible trek difficult. Serving God can be challenging, too. But none of His assignments are beyond our abilities to finish. Each trek gives you an opportunity to improve your showing. In the next journey, we will explore one of the ways Jesus brought His message of salvation to the world.

> *"As for us, the LORD is our God,*
> *and we have not forsaken him. . . .*
> *God is with us; he is our leader."*
> 2 CHRONICLES 13:10, 12

# BIBLE

# TREK

## MASTERPIECES OF SIMPLICITY

■■■■

Ready for some more instruction? As a teacher, one of the problems Jesus faced was the vast cultural and educational differences in His audience members. Galileans and Judeans, few of whom had traveled beyond their country's borders, viewed their world through eyes limited in experience. But His message would be carried to all parts of the world—to people even more backward and superstitious, to self-satisfied citizens of Imperial Rome, to people of ancient Greece with its competing philosophies, to the more experienced and educated people of our day.

### CAPTAIN'S LOG

What Jesus taught would become part of the Gospels to be passed down to our generation. How could He ensure that people of different cultures and languages would understand His message? One way He taught was in simple true-to-life stories. In this Bible trek you will investigate some of these stories, which are better known by the name used in this Bible verse.

"I will open my mouth with a _____; I will utter hidden things."

**1.** Jesus said a person who hears His words and "puts them into practice is like a _____ man who built his house on the _____" (two words).

**2.** The woman who lit a lamp and swept her house was looking for what?

   a. a pearl of great price
   b. a silver coin

**3.** The parables about people who lost things and found them illustrate that there is rejoicing in heaven over what event?

**4.** True or False: When the weeds sown by an enemy ended up sprouting with the good seeds, the servants were told to immediately pull the weeds up and burn them.

**5.** Which parable did Jesus tell during the Sermon on the Mount in Matthew 5–7?

    a. the sower, seeds, and soils
    b. the wise and foolish builders
    c. the good Samaritan
    d. the Pharisee and the tax collector

**6.** What type of plant grew from a small seed and became large enough for birds to perch in its branches?

**7.** What phrase begins each of these parables about hidden treasure, a valuable pearl, and the yeast?

    a. "a prophet of the Lord is like. . ."
    b. "a sinner who repents is like. . ."
    c. "the kingdom of heaven is like. . ."
    d. "the work of the evil one is like. . ."

**8.** Jesus told the parable of the Good Samaritan in answer to the question, "And who is my _____?"

**9.** The man who was helped by the Samaritan was on the road from Jerusalem to what city?

**10.** How did the Samaritan transport the injured man to the inn?

a. in a chariot
b. on a mat carried by four friends
c. on his donkey
d. on his shoulders

**11.** In the parable of the ten virgins, what did the foolish virgins run out of?

**12.** True or False: The parable of the persistent widow who eventually received justice from the judge illustrates that one should pray and never give up.

**13.** In the parable of the Pharisee and tax collector, Jesus said, "For all those who exalt themselves will be _____, and those who _____ themselves will be exalted" (two words).

**14.** What dilemma did the rich farmer with an abundant harvest face?

a. how to divide the inheritance among his seven sons
b. how to store the surplus grain
c. who should receive the excess of his harvest
d. how to fill the banquet hall for the celebration feast

**15.** True or False: In the parable of the workers in the vineyard, workers were hired throughout the day and were paid based on the number of hours they worked.

# BLACK HOLE:

In the parable of the great banquet, what statement was *not* used as a reason to be excused from the feast?

a. I just got married.
b. I must bury my father.
c. I must go see a field I have bought
d. I must try some oxen I have bought

## VOYAGE 23

## ANSWERS

"parable" **(Psalm 78:2)**

1. "wise," "rock" **(Matthew 7:24)**
2. b. a silver coin (Luke 15:8)
3. "one sinner who repents" **(Luke 15:10)**
4. False—the servants were told to wait until the harvest (Matthew 13:27–30)
5. b. the wise and foolish builders (Matthew 7:24–27)
6. mustard (Matthew 13:31)
7. c. "the kingdom of heaven is like. . ." **(Matthew 13:33, 44–45)**
8. "neighbor" **(Luke 10:29)**
9. Jericho (Luke 10:30)
10. c. on his donkey (Luke 10:34)
11. oil for their lamps (Matthew 25:3, 8)
12. True (Luke 18:1)
13. "humbled," "humble" **(Luke 18:14)**
14. b. how to store the surplus grain (Luke 12:16–17)
15. False—all were paid the same (Matthew 20:12)

Black Hole: b. I must bury my father (Luke 14:18–20)

## VOYAGE 23

# WELCOME TO YOUR DEEP SPACE DESTINATION

So how did you do? Did you glean wisdom from the questions about farming parables?

Jesus' stories were based on actual everyday events of those who listened to Him. Seeds that failed to take root, a son who wasted his money, a man on the way to Jericho who was beaten senseless by thieves—these were trials they experienced in daily life. Jesus focused on people and on human qualities. Because of that, the passage of time did not date His parables. Their meanings are still clear today, even after more than 2,000 years.

When Jesus' public ministry began, He was described in the Gospel of Luke as being a teacher (Luke 4:15). He did not teach with parables alone. He also taught by example and by showing His love. After a time to recharge the thrusters, make ready to continue on your next Bible trek. You'll be seeing the compassionate side of Jesus and His love for others.

> *We know also that the Son of God has come*
> *and has given us understanding,*
> *so that we may know him who is true.*
> *And we are in him who is true by being*
> *in his Son Jesus Christ.*
> *He is the true God and eternal life.*
> 1 JOHN 5:20

# BIBLE
# TREK

# VOYAGE 24

## LEGACY OF LOVE

Ready for the next leg of your adventure? In this trek, you will explore something that's more powerful than faith and hope alone. Read on!

Although plainly spoken and simply told, Jesus' parables were not always understood. He had to explain the parable of the sower to His disciples. Other stories must have caused some people to feel uncomfortable. One example is the parable of the Good Samaritan. Jews would never have cast a Samaritan, a member of a people despised by Jews, as the hero of a story that forever linked the word *good* with Samaritan.

### CAPTAIN'S LOG

Words alone can be powerful, but actions tend to speak louder. Jesus followed His sermons and parables with real-life examples of the essential characteristics of God and His Son. In this trek, you will explore some of the ways that He demonstrated the attribute revealed in the Bible verse below.

"This is how we know what _____ is: Jesus Christ laid down his life for us. And we ought to lay down our lives for our brothers and sisters."

**1.** "Surely he took up our pain and bore our suffering, yet we considered him punished by God, stricken by him, and _____."

**2.** "He was despised and rejected by mankind, a man of _____, and familiar with pain."

**3.** Why did Jesus feed the 5,000?

   a. as a sign to the Pharisees
   b. because He felt sorry for them
   c. to do a notable miracle
   d. to establish His dominion

**4.** At the feeding of the 5,000, by what means of transportation did Jesus arrive at the solitary place?

   a. by boat
   b. by miraculous transportation
   c. on a donkey
   d. on foot

**5.** True or False: The multitude was fed at midday.

**6.** "So they sat down in groups of _____ and fifties."

**7.** How many basketfuls of leftover food were taken up?

**8.** When Jesus healed the man with the shriveled hand on the Sabbath day, how did the Pharisees and teachers of the law react?

    a. they said, "Surely this is the son of God"

    b. they were furious

**9.** True or False: The Pharisees reproached the people who brought little children to Jesus.

**10.** What did Jesus say belonged to such as the little children?

**11.** Blind Bartimaeus sat by the roadside near what city?

**12.** Bartimaeus called Jesus the Son of
_____.

**13.** After receiving his sight, what did Bartimaeus do?

    a. followed Jesus
    b. shouted and leaped for joy
    c. took all he owned and offered it at the temple
    d. walked into the city to show himself to the priest

**14.** Before Jesus healed the ten lepers, they stood at a distance and called, saying, "Jesus, Master, have _____ on us!"

**15.** From what region was the one leper who thanked Jesus?

   a. Ethiopia
   b. Galilee
   c. Phoenicia
   d. Samaria

# BLACK HOLE:

When Jesus healed the sick at Capernaum, the words that Matthew quoted—"He took up our infirmities and bore our diseases"—were from the writings of what Old Testament prophet?

## VOYAGE 24

■ ■ ■ ■ ■ ■ ■

### ANSWERS

"love" (**1 John 3:16**)

1. "afflicted" (**Isaiah 53:4**)
2. "suffering" (**Isaiah 53:3**)
3. b. because He felt sorry for them (Mark 6:34)
4. a. by boat (Mark 6:32)
5. False—at evening (Mark 6:35)
6. "hundreds" (**Mark 6:40**)
7. 12 (Mark 6:43)
8. b. they were furious (Luke 6:11)
9. False—His disciples reproached them (Mark 10:13)
10. "the kingdom of God" (**Mark 10:14**)
11. Jericho (Mark 10:46)
12. David (Mark 10:48)
13. a. followed Jesus (Mark 10:52)
14. "pity" (**Luke 17:13**)
15. d. Samaria (Luke 17:16)

Black Hole: Isaiah (**Matthew 8:17**)

## VOYAGE 24

■■■■■■■

## WELCOME TO YOUR DEEP SPACE DESTINATION

The Legacy of Love Bible trek explored the details of only a few of the more than 30 miracles that demonstrated Jesus' authority. The Gospel of John called a miracle a sign. A *sign* points to something greater. The miracles that Jesus performed pointed to Him as one with power over nature itself. He also did them to show His compassion. He fed the 5,000, not to dazzle them with a miracle, but because He had concern for the people.

Remember to total your points. How did you do? Facing the challenge of each new Bible trek takes staying power. When you complete each trek, you can congratulate yourself because you have willingly faced a test of your Bible knowledge. The challenge of your next Bible trek begins shortly. Not everyone embraced Jesus' message, especially those in power who felt threatened by His growing acceptance as one who spoke with authority.

*They refused to listen and failed to remember*
*the miracles you performed among them. . . .*
*But you are a forgiving God, gracious and compassionate,*
*slow to anger and abounding in love.*
NEHEMIAH 9:17

# BIBLE

# TREK

# VOYAGE 25

## RAGE AGAINST THE CHOSEN ONE

Feeling challenged after that last voyage? You'll need all the Bible knowledge you can muster for this next trek.

Words are pale substitutes for actions. What we see always triumphs over what we hear. Jesus spoke words of love, and He followed them up with real-life examples of love. His words were captions on the living portrait of His life. People in Galilee and Judea listened to Jesus and accepted Him as a prophet and teacher. Those in authority resented His growing favor with the people.

### CAPTAIN'S LOG

In this Bible trek you will trace out the growing frustration of the religious leaders as they tried to silence Jesus of Nazareth. They attacked Him in every way they could imagine—they assailed His teachings, His character, and His associates. The Old Testament foresaw that He would face opponents.

"Those who hate me without _____ outnumber the hairs of my head."

1. In Psalms, David refers to the Messiah as a priest forever in the order of what Old Testament person?

2. The teachers of the law said of Jesus, "He is possessed by Beelzebul! By the prince of _____ he is driving out _____" (same word).

3. In what city did the people intend to throw Jesus from a cliff after He read from Isaiah and said that the scripture was fulfilled in their hearing?

4. Jesus told His disciples, "_____ have dens and birds have nests, but the Son of Man has no place to lay his head."

5. True or False: The only place where the people honored Jesus was in His hometown.

**6.** When Jesus asked the Pharisees, "Whose son is the Messiah?" what did they reply?

   a. Moses
   b. Adam
   c. the I AM
   d. David

**7.** "The _____ said to my _____: 'Sit at my right hand until I put your enemies under your feet'" (same word).

**8.** True or False: Gamaliel was the high priest who schemed with the chief priests and elders to arrest Jesus.

**9.** With whom was Jesus eating when He answered criticism by saying that it was not the healthy who needed a doctor but the sick?

**10.** Before Peter was brought before the Sanhedrin, what public miracle did he do in Jesus' name, giving him the opportunity to preach to the people in Solomon's Colonnade?

**11.** To what city does Peter refer when he says, "Herod and Pontius Pilate met together with the Gentiles and the people of Israel in this city to conspire against your holy servant Jesus"?

**12.** In what book of the Old Testament are these words found: "Why do the nations conspire and the peoples plot in vain? The kings of earth rise up and the rulers band together against the LORD and against his anointed"?

  a. Daniel
  b. Isaiah
  c. Micah
  d. Psalms

**13.** In Acts, Peter and _____ were brought before the Sanhedrin and told not to teach about Jesus.

**14.** Shortly before he was stoned, who said, "You stiff-necked people! . . . Was there ever a prophet your ancestors did not persecute?"

**15.** In the New Testament, who explained to the Ethiopian the scripture "He was led like a sheep to the slaughter"?

# BLACK HOLE:

The chief priests and Pharisees told Nicodemus that a prophet does not come from what part of Israel?

    a. Judea
    b. Samaria
    c. Gaza
    d. Galilee

## VOYAGE 25

■ ■ ■ ■ ■ ■ ■

### ANSWERS

"reason" (**Psalm 69:4**)

1. Melchizedek (Psalm 110:4)
2. "demons," "demons" (**Mark 3:22**)
3. Nazareth (Luke 4:16, 21, 29)
4. "Foxes" (**Luke 9:58**)
5. False—they did not honor Him there (Mark 6:1–6)
6. d. David (Matthew 22:41–42)
7. "Lord," "Lord" (**Matthew 22:44**)
8. False—the high priest was Caiaphas (Matthew 26:3–4)
9. tax collectors and sinners (Mark 2:13–17)
10. Peter healed a lame beggar (Acts 3:6–8, 13)
11. Jerusalem (**Acts 4:16, 27**)
12. d. Psalms (**Psalm 2:1–2**)
13. John (Acts 4:13–18)
14. Stephen (**Acts 7:51–52**, 55)
15. Philip (**Acts 8:30–32**)

Black Hole: d. Galilee (John 7:45, 52)

# VOYAGE 25

## WELCOME TO YOUR DEEP SPACE DESTINATION

How did you do on that last danger-filled adventure? Did you come out unscathed or limp back into port? Did you encounter friends or foes?

The enemies of Jesus questioned why He ate with sinners, why He didn't fast, whether the baptism of John was from God or man. When each of His answers crushed their faultfinding, the religious leaders became even more determined to destroy Him.

When they could neither silence nor discredit Jesus, they took the fateful step of scheming to kill Him. They said He claimed to be the Messiah, the Son of God—a charge that served a dual purpose. Under Jewish law they could convict Him of being guilty of blasphemy. Under Roman law He would be guilty of treason by claiming to be king of the Jews.

Jesus was, in fact, the Messiah and Son of God. Even death could not hold the Prince of Glory down. The next Bible trek takes us beyond the great oblivion of death to the resurrection of Jesus.

> *I keep my eyes always on the LORD.*
> *With him at my right hand,*
> *I will not be shaken.*
> PSALM 16:8

# BIBLE
# TREK

# VOYAGE 26

## BEYOND THE GREAT OBLIVION

In this trek we will explore the final days of Jesus on earth.

Jewish religious leaders, Roman government officials, and one of Jesus' own apostles had a hand in the events that resulted in the Lord's execution. To appease leaders who had stirred up the crowd, Pilate sentenced Jesus to death by crucifixion—the usual Roman sentence for criminals. Jesus died before the day was out. Check the Captain's Log for the next challenge.

### CAPTAIN'S LOG

The evening Jesus died, Joseph of Arimathea buried the Lord's body in a cavelike tomb. Although most of the disciples had fled, women stood nearby and saw where He had been buried. On Sunday morning they came to anoint Jesus' body but found the stone rolled away and the tomb empty. The Bible verse below shows that prophets had foreseen what would happen next.

"You will not abandon me to the realm of the dead, nor will you let your faithful one see _____."

**1.** Isaiah writes, "He will swallow up _____ forever."

**2.** After saying, "I am the resurrection and the life. The one who believes in me will live, even though they die; and whoever lives by believing in me will never die," who did Jesus ask, "Do you believe this?"

   a. Herod, while Jesus was on trial
   b. Martha, sister of Lazarus
   c. Peter
   d. Thomas, who doubted

**3.** According to the Gospel of John, who else was with Joseph of Arimathea when Joseph buried Jesus?

   a. Barnabas
   b. Cleopas
   c. John, a disciple, not the apostle
   d. Nicodemus

**4.** Who rolled the big stone across the tomb after Jesus' body had been placed in it?

   a. chief priests and Pharisees
   b. Joseph of Arimathea
   c. soldiers who crucified Him
   d. temple guards

**5.** True or False: Mary Magdalene was one of the women who saw where Jesus' body was laid.

**6.** Why did the women who prepared spices for Jesus' body delay until the first day of the week before going to the tomb?

**7.** On the first day of the week, as the women went to anoint Jesus' body with spices, what question did they ask each other?

**8.** The two men in glowing clothes at the empty tomb asked the women, "Why do you look for the _____ among the _____?" (two words).

**9.** How did the disciples react when Mary Magdalene and the other women told them Jesus was alive?

 a. with disbelief
 b. with rejoicing

**10.** True or False: The two men on the road to Emmaus who walked and talked with Jesus never realized who He was.

**11.** When the disciples gathered on the evening of the first day of the week after Jesus' resurrection, why did they have the doors locked?

**12.** Thomas, who said, "Unless I see the nail marks in his hands. . .I will not believe," was a disciple of Jesus but not an apostle.

**13.** After Jesus arose, who did He ask three times "Do you love me?"

**14.** Jesus said, "Therefore go and make disciples of all _____, baptizing them in the name of the Father and of the Son and of the Holy Spirit."

**15** Jesus was taken up into heaven in the vicinity of what small city?

# BLACK HOLE:

After Jesus' resurrection when He directs the disciples to let down their net on the other side of the ship, how many fish did they catch?

## VOYAGE 26

■■■■■■■

### ANSWERS

"decay" (**Psalm 16:10**)

1. "death" (**Isaiah 25:8**)
2. b. Martha, sister of Lazarus (**John 11**:21, **25–26**)
3. d. Nicodemus (John 19:38–42)
4. b. Joseph of Arimathea (Matthew 27:57–60)
5. True (Mark 15:47)
6. they rested on the Sabbath (Luke 23:56)
7. "Who will roll the stone away from the entrance of the tomb?" (**Mark 16:3**)
8. "living," "dead" (**Luke 24:5**)
9. a. with disbelief (Luke 24:11)
10. False—"their eyes were opened and they recognized him" (**Luke 24:31**)
11. they feared the Jewish leaders (John 20:19)
12. False—he was one of the Twelve (**John 20:24–25**)
13. Peter (**John 21:17**)
14. "nations" (**Matthew 28:19**)
15. Bethany (Luke 24:50–51)

Black Hole: 153 (John 21:6, 11)

# VOYAGE 26

■ ■ ■ ■ ■ ■ ■

## WELCOME TO YOUR DEEP SPACE DESTINATION

How did you fare on that amazing adventure? Did you complete it fearlessly?

During the 40 days from the time of His resurrection to His ascension, one of Jesus' most frequent statements to His apostles and disciples was "Fear not." At the time of His arrest, their courage had deserted them, and they had fled in fear. After seeing the risen Christ, the disciples regained their courage. They dared to boldly proclaim His teachings in Jerusalem at the temple. Courageous speakers such as Peter and John preached the message that God raised Jesus to life.

In the next Bible trek, we'll see the revitalized apostles and disciples determined to carry out Jesus' final command. Rather than the sacrifice of a lamb at Passover for the sins of the Jewish people, the Lamb of God had been sacrificed for the sins of all people everywhere. It now becomes the responsibility of the apostles and disciples of Jesus to take that message to all nations.

*I want to know Christ—yes, to know the power*
*of his resurrection and participation in his sufferings,*
*becoming like him in his death, and so, somehow,*
*attaining to the resurrection from the dead.*
PHILIPPIANS 3:10–11

# BIBLE

# TREK

# VOYAGE 27

■ ■ ■ ■ ■ ■ ■

## GRACE UNBOUNDED

Did you do well exploring the events during the last 40 days of Jesus' earthly ministry? It's time to power up for your next trek. For a time after Jesus ascended, His message continued to be brought to the Jews alone. Some believed that only by keeping all the laws of the Old Testament covenant could a person enter into a relationship with God. In this view, Christianity was merely a new sect of Judaism. The Captain's Log reveals the growing understanding of how Christianity was to be shared with all nations.

### CAPTAIN'S LOG

In Jesus' parable of the feast (Luke 14:16–24), those first called failed to respond, so the poor, blind, and lame were invited. This illustrated God's intention to welcome all. Jesus' statements in the New Testament and the actions of the apostles would demonstrate that Christianity was open to everyone. In fact, Old Testament prophets also spoke about this aspect of God's plan, as shown by the Bible verse below.

"I will also make you a light for the _____, that my salvation may reach to the ends of the earth."

**1.** The Lord said, "The days are coming. . . when I will make a new _____ with the people of Israel and with the people of Judah."

**2.** "I will put my law in their _____ and write it on their _____. I will be their God, and they will be my people" (two words).

**3.** When Jesus was presented at the temple, what was the name of the righteous and devout man who said, "For my eyes have seen your salvation. . .a light for revelation to the Gentiles, and the glory of your people Israel."

   a. Ananias
   b. Simeon
   c. Stephen
   d. Zacchaeus

**4.**  To whom in the Old Testament did God say, "Through your offspring all peoples on earth will be blessed"?

    a. Abraham
    b. Adam
    c. David
    d. Moses

**5.** To whom did the Lord say: "Go [to the blind Paul]! This man is my chosen instrument to proclaim my name to the Gentiles and their kings and to the people of Israel"?

**6.** In what city did Cornelius live?

**7.** What was Cornelius's profession?

**8.** The angel told Cornelius that his prayers and what other actions had "come up as a memorial offering before God"?

**9.** The angel told Cornelius that Peter could be found in what city?

    a. Capernaum
    b. Jericho
    c. Jerusalem
    d. Joppa

**10.** When the voice in Peter's vision told him to kill and eat the unclean animals, how did Peter respond?

    a. he held his hand up in fear and asked that the vision be taken away
    b. he said, "I am the Lord's servant"
    c. he said, "I surely shall do so"
    d. he said, "Surely not, Lord!"

**11.** True or False: Peter told Cornelius that it was against Jewish law "for a Jew to associate with or visit a Gentile."

**12.** Paul and Barnabas met with the apostles and elders in Jerusalem to settle what question?

**13.** At the conference, who spoke last and said, "It is my judgment, therefore, that we should not make it difficult for the Gentiles"?

a. Barnabas
b. James
c. Paul
d. Peter

**14.** When Paul and Barnabas applied the Old Testament phrase "a light for the Gentiles" to themselves, who were they quoting?

**15.** Paul quotes Isaiah as saying, "The Root of _____ will spring up, one who will arise to rule over the nations; in him the Gentiles will hope."

# BLACK HOLE:

At the end of the Jerusalem conference, the apostles and elders sent a letter by Paul and his companions to what major Gentile city?

## VOYAGE 27

■ ■ ■ ■ ■ ■ ■

### ANSWERS

"Gentiles" (**Isaiah 49:6**)

1. "covenant" (**Jeremiah 31:31**)
2. "minds," "hearts" (**Jeremiah 31:33**)
3. b. Simeon (**Luke 2**:25, **30, 32**)
4. a. Abraham (**Acts 3:25**)
5. Ananias (**Acts 9:15**)
6. Caesarea (Acts 10:1)
7. soldier or centurion (Acts 10:1)
8. "gifts to the poor" (**Acts 10:4**)
9. d. Joppa (Acts 10:5)
10. d. he said, "Surely not, Lord!" (**Acts 10:14**)
11. True (**Acts 10:27–28**)
12. whether Gentiles had to be circumcised to be saved (Acts 15:1–2)
13. b. James (**Acts 15:13–19**)
14. Isaiah (**Isaiah 49:6**)
15. "Jesse" (**Romans 15:12**)

Black Hole: Antioch (Acts 15:22–23)

# VOYAGE 27

■ ■ ■ ■ ■ ■ ■

## WELCOME TO YOUR DEEP SPACE DESTINATION

Peter was in Joppa when the vision of the animals let down from heaven came to him. At first Peter was puzzled. Why would God tell him to kill and eat animals forbidden as food under Jewish law? Later, after traveling to Caesarea, he understood the meaning and welcomed Cornelius into Christian fellowship. Nothing prevented believing Gentiles such as Cornelius from accepting Christ. But some disciples in Jerusalem insisted the Gentile believers must first become Jews to be acceptable. Peter disagreed, as did Paul and James. The result of the Jerusalem conference was conclusive. Observing the Law of Moses was not necessary for Gentile Christians to come into Christian fellowship.

It is time to move on, so prepare for the next challenge. From now on your Bible trek will take you farther and farther from Jerusalem and the center of Judaism. You will join "away teams" who take the message of salvation into the very heart of the Roman Empire.

*I am not ashamed of the gospel, because it is the power*
*of God that brings salvation to everyone who believes:*
*first to the Jew, then to the Gentile.*
*For in the gospel the righteousness of God is revealed—*
*a righteousness that is by faith*
*from first to last, just as it is written:*
*"The righteous will live by faith."*
ROMANS 1:16–17

# BIBLE
# TREK

# VOYAGE 28

## AWAY TEAMS

Congratulations on making it this far. When the travel becomes difficult, sharing the experience with another person lightens the load. God recognized the need for teamwork. Daniel's determination to serve God remained strong because he had the comfort of three like-minded friends (Shadrach, Meshach, and Abednego). After Elijah cried out that he alone had not bowed to Baal, God gave Elijah a companion prophet, Elisha. Read the Captain's Log to learn about your next assignment.

### CAPTAIN'S LOG

Jesus more often than not sent teams of individuals to fulfill specific tasks. Paul usually traveled on his missionary efforts with a team of Christians. Members of a team who work well together can strengthen one another. Prepare for a Bible trek that looks at New Testament Bible teams and their assignments.

One missionary team in the New Testament was made up of Paul and Silas and a young believer named _____.

**1.** True or False: When Jesus first sent out the Twelve, He told them to go to all nations.

**2.** Jesus also told the Twelve, "I am sending you out like sheep among _____."

**3.** When Jesus sent out the Seventy-Two, what did He tell them?

  a. "speak clearly without figures of speech"
  b. "the harvest is plentiful, but the workers are few"
  c. "the sign of Jonah will follow you"
  d. "you are My friends if you do what I command"

**4.** When Jesus entered Jerusalem during the week before His betrayal, how many disciples did He send to get the colt for Him to ride?

**5.** How many disciples did Jesus send to arrange for the room for the Passover meal?

**6.** Who was the one chosen to be numbered with the 11 apostles to replace Judas?

    a. Joseph
    b. Matthias

**7.** In Acts, seven men full of the Spirit and wisdom were chosen so the apostles would not have to do what?

**8.** Barnabas traveled to Tarsus and brought Saul (Paul) to what city where believers were first called Christians.

    a. Antioch
    b. Capernaum
    c. Cappadocia
    d. Damascus

**9.** Paul's first missionary partner was Barnabas, a name meaning "son of
_____."

**10.** Paul, Barnabas, and John Mark began their first missionary journey by going to what island where Sergius Paulus was proconsul?

a. Crete
b. Cyprus
c. Malta
d. Rhodes

**11.** After the first missionary journey, Paul did not think it wise to take John Mark to revisit churches because John Mark had _____ him in Pamphylia.

**12.** Who does the Bible say was related to John Mark?

a. Barnabas
b. Paul

**13.** Instead of Barnabas, who accompanied Paul at the start of his second missionary journey?

**14.** What Greek believer does Paul call, "my true son in our common faith"? (Hint: one of Paul's letters is written to him.)

**15.** Who told Timothy, "Get Mark and bring him with you, because he is helpful to me in my ministry"?

    a. Aquila
    b. Barnabas
    c. Paul
    d. Peter

# BLACK HOLE:

To Timothy, Paul wrote, "I am reminded of your sincere faith, which first lived in your grandmother _____ and in your mother _____." (two names).

## VOYAGE 28

■■■■■■■

### ANSWERS

Timothy (Acts 15:40; 16:1–3)

1. False—"to the lost sheep of Israel" (**Matthew 10**:5–**6**)
2. "wolves" (**Matthew 10:16**)
3. b. "the harvest is plentiful, but the workers are few" (**Luke 10**:1–2)
4. two (Mark 11:1–2)
5. two (Mark 14:12–16)
6. b. Matthias (Acts 1:26)
7. wait on tables (Acts 6:1–4)
8. a. Antioch (Acts 11:25–26)
9. "encouragement" (**Acts 4:36**; 13:2–4)
10. b. Cyprus (Acts 13:2–7)
11. deserted (Acts 15:37–38)
12. a. Barnabas (Colossians 4:10)
13. Silas (Acts 15:40)
14. Titus (Galatians 2:3; **Titus 1:4**)
15. c. Paul (**2 Timothy** 1:1–2; **4:11**)

Black Hole: "Lois," "Eunice" (**2 Timothy 1:5**)

## VOYAGE 28

# WELCOME TO YOUR DEEP SPACE DESTINATION

Check your point total for this trek. Did you manage to answer enough questions to be traveling at Light Speed or better?

The New Testament tells of several teams sent by Jesus. Two individuals arranged an upper room for the Passover meal. Three individuals accompanied Jesus to the Mount of Transfiguration (Luke 9:28). Four apostles were working together as fishermen when Jesus called them (Matthew 4:18–22). In Acts 6:1–4, seven men were chosen to serve the Grecian widows. Cornelius sent two servants and a trusted soldier to call for Peter (Acts 10:7). Six believers accompanied Paul to Caesarea (Acts 11:12). Do you see the advantage of teamwork?

The next Bible trek will begin when Paul has a vision that diverts him from his planned trip into Rome's easternmost province and into another one that takes him closer to Rome itself.

> *Therefore if you have any encouragement*
> *from being united with Christ. . .*
> *then make my joy complete by being like-minded,*
> *having the same love,*
> *being one in spirit and of one mind.*
> PHILIPPIANS 2:1–2

# BIBLE

# TREK

# VOYAGE 29

## PERSISTENCE OF VISION

Ready to ship out on a new adventure? In this voyage we'll be traveling with Paul.

After he was converted and then met the apostles in Jerusalem, Paul traveled to Tarsus. Barnabas brought him to Antioch in Syria (Acts 11:25–26). Later, with John Mark, they began the first missionary journey, going first to Cyprus and ending up in Antioch.

On the second journey, Paul left with Silas (Acts 15:40) and was joined by Timothy (Acts 16:1). Afterward Paul returned to Antioch.

### CAPTAIN'S LOG

In the second missionary journey, the action of the Holy Spirit and Paul's subsequent vision caused him to change his itinerary. Rather than going farther northeast of Lystra, he headed westward. During his third missionary journey, Paul revisits many of the churches he'd previously established.

The Holy Spirit prevented Paul, Silas, and Timothy from "preaching the word in the province of
_____."

**1.** The man in Paul's vision begged him to "come over to _____."

**2.** True or False: Because Philippi was a Roman colony and a leading city of that district, Paul avoiding traveling there.

**3.** Paul was in what city when he had the vision of the man calling him?

    a. Alexandria
    b. Pontus
    c. Thyatira
    d. Troas

**4.** True or False: At Philippi Paul met Lydia, a woman who had a spirit by which she predicted the future.

**5.** When Paul and Silas were in prison in Philippi, why was the jailer about to kill himself?

**6.** After encountering angry mobs in Philippi, Thessalonica, and Berea, the believers sent Paul to Athens, a city filled with _____.

**7.** While in Athens, what group began to debate with Paul?

a. Stoic philosophers and Epicureans
b. jealous Jews and merchants of the marketplace
c. the magistrates and officials of the city
d. the makers of gold and silver idols

**8.** Paul told the Athenians, God "does not live in temples built by _____ _____" (two words).

**9.** After leaving Athens for Corinth, Paul met Aquila and Priscilla, who had been ordered from Rome by what leader?

a. Augustus
b. Claudius
c. Nero
d. Tiberius

**10.** After traveling to Ephesus, Aquila and Priscilla met Apollos and "explained to him the way of God more _____."

**11.** When the seven sons of Sceva tried to imitate Paul's miracles, the evil spirit said, "_____ I know, and Paul I know about, but who are you?"

**12.** Demetrius, the silversmith who made images of Artemis, led a riot in what city?

a. Athens
b. Corinth
c. Ephesus
d. Rome

**13.** In Troas, what happened to cause Eutychus to be "picked up dead"?

**14.** At Ephesus, Paul said, "My only aim is to finish the _____ and complete the _____ the Lord Jesus has given me" (two words).

**15.** To which city did Paul *not* write a letter that is part of the New Testament?

    a. Athens
    b. Corinth
    c. Ephesus
    d. Galatia

# BLACK HOLE:

Paul's plea for Onesimus was directed to which of his "fellow workers"?

    a. Philemon
    b. Tertius
    c. Timothy
    d. Titus

# VOYAGE 29

■■■■■

## ANSWERS

"Asia" (**Acts 16:6**)

1.  "Macedonia" (**Acts 16:9**)
2.  False—he stayed there several days (Acts 16:12)
3.  d. Troas (Acts 16:8–9)
4.  False—she dealt in purple cloth (Acts 16:14)
5.  "he thought the prisoners had escaped" (**Acts 16:27**)
6.  idols (Acts 17:16)
7.  a. Stoic philosophers and Epicureans (Acts 17:18)
8.  "human hands" (**Acts 17:24**)
9.  b. Claudius (Acts 18:2)
10. "adequately" (**Acts 18:26**)
11. "Jesus" (**Acts 19:15**)
12. c. Ephesus (Acts 19:24–29)
13. he fell from a window (**Acts 20:9**)
14. "race," "task" (**Acts 20:24**)
15. a. Athens; he wrote letters to the Corinthians, Ephesians, and Galatians

Black Hole: Philemon (**Philemon 1:10, 24**)

# VOYAGE 29

## WELCOME TO YOUR DEEP SPACE DESTINATION

Perhaps you found some of these questions difficult. Certainly Paul encountered challenges during his journeys. In 2 Corinthians 11:23–28, he lists some of the dangers he faced. Paul kept the faith in Jesus that carried him through perilous missions. Faith is important, but even more important is in whom we put our faith.

Paul was directed by the vision to go to the Roman providence of Macedonia—part of which was Greece but was ruled by Rome. The third missionary journey began in Acts 19 with Paul spending most of his time in Ephesus, Macedonia, and Greece. He'd ended his previous journeys at Antioch. This time he traveled directly to Jerusalem. He was arrested at the temple and defended himself in four separate trials—before the Sanhedrin, before Felix and Festus who were Roman governors, and before King Agrippa. Eventually he was placed under guard and boarded a ship that set sail to Rome. There he would stand trial before Caesar. Through it all, he kept his faith and trust in Christ.

*How, then, can they call
on the one they have not believed in?
And how can they believe
in the one of whom they have not heard?
And how can they hear without someone preaching to them?*
ROMANS 10:14

# BIBLE
# TREK

# VOYAGE 30

■■■■■■ ■■

## DESTINY'S END

Sometimes we become so certain of our own position that we become blind to the fact we have lost our way. During his early life, Saul blindly pursued his goal of persecuting Christian believers. But then, in a life-changing encounter on the road to Damascus, Paul saw the light. There his haughty nature was replaced with one of Christian love. He chose to follow the course God revealed to him. Like Paul, no matter where our travels take us, if we follow the Lord's vision for us rather than our own, God will be with us.

Your trek through the Bible is almost over. The final destination is right ahead. Read the Captain's Log to learn your final orders.

## CAPTAIN'S LOG

Prepare for a long journey this time. Under guard, Paul sailed across the Mediterranean Sea in what became a fourth missionary trip. He was swept up in a terrific storm before arriving safely at Rome. The book of Acts ends there, a fitting conclusion to Paul's travels.

The apostle to the _____ was in Rome, the chief city of the _____ world.

**1.** After Paul's arrest in Jerusalem, why did the centurion hesitate to flog Paul?

**2.** After being struck while before the Sanhedrin, Paul said, "God will strike you, you _____ wall!"

**3.** What information about Paul's safety did Paul's nephew bring to the Roman commander?

**4.** The Roman commander called for soldiers, horsemen, and spearmen to safely take Paul to Governor Felix in the city of _____.

**5.** As Paul spoke of the judgment to come, Felix became fearful and said, "You may leave. When I find it _____, I will send for you."

**6.** Festus told Paul, "You have appealed to _____. To _____ you will go!" (same word).

**7.** Which of Paul's inquisitors said, "Do you think that in such a short time you can persuade me to be a Christian?"

   a. Ananias, the high priest
   b. Felix
   c. Festus
   d. King Agrippa

**8.** How did the centurion named Julius treat Paul during the voyage to Rome?

   a. kept him in chains below deck
   b. showed Paul kindness

**9.** After landing at Fair Havens, Paul predicted a disastrous voyage if they continued, but the centurion "followed the advice of the pilot and the _____ of the ship."

**10.** As the ship sailed along the coast of Crete, it was struck by a wind of hurricane force known by what name?

    a. blustering wind
    b. Jonah storm
    c. Northeaster
    d. red-morning tempest

**11.** For how many days had those on the ship been in suspense of the storm and without food?

**12.** Why did the soldiers cut the ropes and let the lifeboat drift away?

**13.** How many people died in the shipwreck?

**14.** How did the islanders of Malta treat those who survived the shipwreck?

   a. they demonstrated extraordinary kindness

   b. they were suspicious and refused to aid them

**15.** True or False: The Jewish leaders in Rome told Paul, "We are convinced we should not listen to you."

# BLACK HOLE:

For how many years had Paul been in Rome when Acts ends?

# VOYAGE 30

## ANSWERS

Gentiles, Gentile (Romans 11:13)

1. because Paul was a Roman citizen (Acts 22:25)
2. "whitewashed" (**Acts 23:3**)
3. 40 Jews were plotting to kill Paul (Acts 23:16–17, 21)
4. Caesarea (Acts 23:23–24)
5. "convenient" (**Acts 24:25**)
6. "Caesar," "Caesar" (**Acts 25:12**)
7. d. King Agrippa (**Acts 26:28**)
8. b. showed Paul kindness (Acts 27:1–3)
9. "owner" (**Acts 27:8–11**)
10. c. Northeaster (Acts 27:14)
11. 14 (Acts 27:33)
12. Paul said they must stay with the ship to be saved (Acts 27:30–32)
13. none (Acts 27:44)
14. a. they demonstrated extraordinary kindness (Acts 28:2)
15. False—they said, "We want to hear what your views are" (**Acts 28:17–22**)

Black Hole: two (Acts 28:30)

# VOYAGE 30

## WELCOME TO YOUR DEEP SPACE DESTINATION

You've completed 30 treks and returned safely to your deep-space destination. In addition to the fun and excitement of interesting voyages, you've gained an understanding of the trials that Bible believers faced in their daily lives. Some left comfortable homes to travel to a land showed to them by God. Others dealt with a nemesis whose goals were contrary to their own and to those of the Lord. In addition you've made Temporal Jumps from passages in the Old Testament to the corresponding events in the New Testament. Count yourself fortunate to have the opportunity to explore the Bible in this entertaining and educational way.

Like the voyages in Bible Trek, you'll face events in your life that may feel like a Tractor Beam holding you back. With the right attitude, prayer, Bible study, and faith in the Savior, you'll race along at Maximum Warp Speed. Still more great voyages of spiritual discovery await you in the Bible. Enjoy daily Bible reading and think about what you read. Apply God's love and grace to your life to overcome whatever obstacles you encounter during your personal journey.

> *"For I know the plans I have for you," declares the* LORD,
> *"plans to prosper you and not to harm you,*
> *plans to give you hope and a future."*
> JEREMIAH 29:11

# ABOUT THE AUTHOR

*John Hudson Tiner,* formerly a science teacher and cartographer (mapmaker), is a freelance writer from Missouri. He is best known for his popular works on science and religion, though he has written in many genres. John and his wife, Jeanene, have two children and eight grandchildren.